GW00891762

HOUSE PLA[N]
JOTTER Dr. D.G. Hessayon

1st Edition 350,000

Other Books in the JOTTER Series:
ROSE JOTTER · VEGETABLE JOTTER

Year:	Location:

pbi PUBLICATIONS · BRITANNICA HOUSE · WALTHAM CROSS · HERTS · ENGLAND

Printed and bound by Hazell Watson and Viney Limited Aylesbury Bucks. England

ISBN 0 903505 26 6

CHAPTER 1

INTRODUCTION

How to use this book

On each page you will find scores of facts to help you with your plants. Check up each time you decide to buy or have a new job to do. On many of the pages there are sections which are printed in blue — these are for you to fill in with your own information. In this way you can build up a permanent record and a useful reminder for next year.

House plants have a special charm which is difficult to explain. In the garden we may walk past a group of begonias or geraniums without really noticing them, but put one in a pot on the windowsill and everything changes. We are delighted when the flowers open and disturbed when the leaves turn yellow. Perhaps the charm is not really difficult to explain. That begonia or geranium in a pot is not merely a plant — it is a pet.

A pet which must rely on you in order to stay alive. For this reason it is vital to choose with care and to learn the correct way to look after your plant companions indoors. The green ones can be expected to survive for years with proper care. The situation with the flowering ones is not so simple — some varieties can live in your home more or less permanently but others are bound to die or become dormant once flowering is over.

This book sets out to tell you the needs and display value of all the common and not-so-common house plants you are likely to find. In addition it will provide you with a record of your successes and failures.

PLANT TYPES

FOLIAGE PLANTS
The backbone of many collections. These are the varieties which are grown for their leaves and/or stems. They can be expected to live permanently under room conditions provided their needs are met. These requirements range from very simple to extremely demanding.

For further details and varieties see pages 6–25.

FLOWERING PLANTS
The colourful highlights of many collections. These are the varieties which are grown for their flowers and/or fruits. Some (Flowering House Plants) can be expected to live permanently under room conditions — the remainder (Temporary Pot Plants) provide a display of limited duration.

For further details and varieties see pages 26–45.

CACTI
The popular spiny plants in many collections. They belong to the family of Succulents which are leafless and are grown for their unusual or attractive stems. These stems bear woolly tufts known as areoles. With proper care many will flower each year.

For further details and varieties see pages 46–49.

THE ENVIRONMENT

SHADE Aglaonema, Aspidistra, Asplenium, Fittonia, Helxine, Philodendron scandens, Sansevieria, Scindapsus (variegation will fade). Any of the Semi-Shade group can be grown here for a month or two; some will survive permanently	**SEMI-SHADE** Aglaonema, Aspidistra, Dracaena fragrans, Dracaena marginata, Fatshedera, Fatsia, Ferns, Ficus pumila, Fittonia, Hedera helix, Helxine, Howea, Maranta, Neanthe, Philodendron scandens, Sansevieria, Scindapsus, Tolmiea
BRIGHT BUT SUNLESS Anthurium, Asparagus, Azalea, Begonia rex, Bromeliads, Chlorophytum, Columnea, Cyclamen, Dieffenbachia, Dizygotheca, Fuchsia, Hedera, Hyacinth, Monstera, Narcissus, Peperomia, Philodendron, Pilea, Schefflera, Scindapsus, Spathiphyllum, Tulipa, Vines, Zygocactus	**SOME DIRECT SUNLIGHT** Beloperone, Capsicum, Chlorophytum, Chrysanthemum, Codiaeum, Cordyline terminalis, Cuphea, Ficus elastica decora, Gynura, Hoya, Impatiens, Nertera, Plumbago, Poinsettia, Saintpaulia, Sansevieria, Solanum, Sparmannia, Tradescantia, Zebrina
SUNNY WINDOW Acacia, Agapanthus, Bougainvillea, Cacti & Succulents, Callistemon, Celosia, Citrus, Coleus, Garden Annuals, Heliotropium, Hibiscus, Hippeastrum, Iresine, Jasminum, Lantana, Nerine, Nerium, Passiflora, Pelargonium, Rosa, Zebrina	**GLASS CONTAINER** Acorus, Calathea, Cocos weddeliana, Codiaeum, Cryptanthus, Dracaena sanderana, smaller Ferns, Ficus pumila, Fittonia, Hedera, Maranta, Neanthe bella, Pellionia, Peperomia, Pilea, Rhoeo, Saintpaulia, Sansevieria, Selaginella
NO HEAT IN WINTER Araucaria, Aspidistra, Beloperone, Cacti & Succulents, Chlorophytum, Cineraria, Clivia, Cyclamen, Fatshedera, Fatsia, Grevillea, Hedera helix, Helxine, Hydrangea, Nertera, Rosa, Saxifraga sarmentosa, Setcreasea, Streptocarpus, Tolmiea	**CENTRAL HEATING IN WINTER** Increase humidity to counteract desert-dry air. Otherwise choose dry air plants such as Aechmea, Billbergia, Cacti & Succulents, Chlorophytum, Dracaena godseffiana, Ficus elastica decora, Grevillea, Nerium, Peperomia, Zebrina

SHAPES

GRASSY PLANTS

Long narrow leaves with a grass-like habit. Few true grasses are offered but there are a few grass-like plants with very narrow leaves (e.g Acorus). Broad-leaved grassy plants are much more popular — e.g Chlorophytum, Narcissus and Billbergia

LEAFY PLANTS

Leaves arise directly out of the compost — no well-defined stem is formed. The leaves neither trail nor form a distinct rosette. Many young plants have this growth habit, but surprisingly few mature ones do — examples are Aspidistra, Caladium and many Ferns

BUSHY PLANTS

Several stems arise out of the compost — the growth habit is neither markedly vertical nor horizontal. They may be small and compact like Pilea or tall and shrubby like Aucuba. A vast number of plants belong here

COLUMNAR PLANTS

Thick vertical stems which are either leafless or bear leaves which do not detract from the column effect. Many Cacti and some Succulents have this shape — typical examples are Cereus peruvianus, Kleinia articulata and Cleistocactus straussii

TREES

A central branched or unbranched stem with leaves which bear relatively short leaf stalks. Some are quite small such as miniature Succulent 'trees'. Others are tall and imposing — examples are Citrus, Polyscias, Podocarpus and Ficus elastica decora

FALSE PALMS

The stem is clothed by leaf bases when young — with the mature plant the trunk is bare and only the crown is crowded with leaves. The effect is distinctly palm-like — examples are Dracaena, Yucca and Pandanus

CLIMBERS

The weak stems are always provided with upright supports. Non-clinging and non-twining varieties need to be attached to these supports. Examples include Stephanotis, Passiflora and Monstera

CLIMBER/TRAILERS

The weak stems are either provided with upright supports or allowed to trail. Many popular varieties belong to this group — including Ficus pumila, Hedera, Philodendron scandens and Scindapsus. Pinch out tips occasionally when grown as trailers

TRAILERS

The weak stems are allowed to hang downwards or creep over the surface of the compost. Most look best in hanging baskets or stood on high pedestals. Examples are Columnea, Nertera and Campanula isophylla

ROSETTES

Leaves form a circular cluster around the central growing point. Some types have a loose rosette of leaves which lie almost horizontally — e.g Saintpaulia and Gloxinia. Others have several layers of tightly-packed leaves — e.g Sempervivum and Echeveria

FUNNEL ROSETTES

A distinct type of rosette — strap-like leaves form a 'vase' which holds rainwater in the natural tropical habitat. Plants are usually large and spreading. A feature of many Bromeliads, such as Aechmea and Vriesea

BALL PLANTS

Leafless stems which are distinctly globular. Nearly all are Cacti — the stem surface may be smooth or covered with hair or spines. Examples are Astrophytum, Ferocactus, Mammillaria, Euphorbia obesa and Echinocactus grusonii

PLANT DISPLAY

Specimen Plant

A Specimen Plant is a foliage or flowering plant grown as a solitary feature. It may be retained in its pot or transplanted into a container. Its purpose is to provide an attractive focal point.

It makes good design sense to display as solitary specimens fine examples of large foliage plants ('Architectural Plants') or bold flowering plants in full bloom. Small and medium-sized foliage plants, however, are usually best grouped together and not kept as isolated pots on shelves and windowsills.

Pot Group

A Pot Group is a collection of plants in pots or individual containers closely grouped to create a massed effect. The pots remain visible as separate units. There are four distinct advantages — the overall effect is bolder than can be achieved with individual pots, small-leaved plants can be used to good effect, damaged parts of plants can be hidden and air humidity around the leaves is increased.

The usual arrangement is to use foliage plants to provide the permanent framework and flowering plants to provide splashes of colour. The dark greens and larger leaves are placed at the back of the group.

Pebble Tray

A useful technique for growing plants which need humid conditions. The tray should be about 2 in. high — add a 1 in. layer of gravel and keep the bottom of this layer wet at all times. Do not let the water cover the top of the gravel.

Vertical Display

The Pot Group is nearly always a horizontal display. The Vertical Group, however, is both easily arranged and can be extremely effective. The traditional version is a corner unit with a pot on each shelf — other variations are a series of hanging baskets or a group of pots in a metal or cane plant stand.

Indoor Garden

An Indoor Garden is a container filled with several plants, in which no pots can be seen. The pots may have been removed or merely hidden from sight.

An Indoor Garden may be five small plants in a bowl or a forest of greenery and flowers in a multi-tiered Planter, but the basic advantages are the same. All the advantages listed for the Pot Group are there, plus the added benefit of creating a 'natural' effect — a true garden is produced.

In a standard Planter the pots are retained so that the plants can be easily lifted out when no longer required. The pots are surrounded by peat. The added benefit here is that excess water runs into the peat at the base and so there is a self-watering effect.

In small containers and hanging baskets take care not to overwater. Also keep a watch for pests and diseases — they are encouraged by close planting.

Terrarium

Fishtank Garden

A Terrarium is a glass or transparent plastic container inside which plants are grown. The top is either naturally restricted or covered with transparent material. A glass-cased garden which opens at the top is known as a Fishtank Garden. A Bottle Garden is made in a container with a restricted opening at the top, and the many attractive glass cases which open at the sides are sold simply as Terraria.

Because draughts are removed and the air is always moist you can grow a wide range of delicate plants. Removal of dead plants often poses a problem — for maximum ease of access choose a Fishtank Garden.

Bottle Garden

Terrarium

CHAPTER 2
VARIETIES

WATER
See pages 52 and 55 for details of the growing and resting periods

	Plentifully
	Moderately
	Sparingly
—	Kept outdoors or not watered indoors

EASY or DIFFICULT
A general guide only — actual ease or difficulty depends on the specific conditions you are able to provide

FAMILY GROUP

Evergreen Foliage Plant	Foliage plant for permanent display
Deciduous or Temporary Foliage Plant	Foliage plant for temporary display
Flowering House Plant	Flowering plant which lives year round in the room
Temporary Pot Plant	Flowering plant for temporary stay in the room

LIGHT

	Maximum direct sunlight
	Morning or evening direct sunlight
	Bright, but no direct sunlight
	Shady, but not dark

WARMTH
Minimum night temperature required to maintain healthy growth

	60–70°F
	50–60°F
	40–50°F

DIMENSIONS
Height and/or leaf size at maturity — bloom size for flowering types. 'Height' in case of trailing plants refers to stem length

AIR HUMIDITY

	Moist air
	Moderately dry air
	Dry air

page 45

VARIETIES

FLOWERING PLANTS

HOUSE PLANT RECORD

Very good-flowered in September

Common name	CONDITIONS REQUIRED					PLANT DETAILS		Variety grown	Year of arrival	Supplier	Performance during the year	Easy or difficult
	Light	Air humidity	Warmth	Growing period	Resting period	Dimensions	Family group					
				▲▲	—	Flowers 2–4 in. long	Temporary Pot Plant	Red	86	Byways G.C.		Moderately easy
Tulip				▲▲▲		Height 1–2 ft Flowers 3 in. across	Flowering House Plant					Easy
Scarborough Lily				▲▲▲		Height 1 ft Flower-heads 4 in. long	Temporary Pot Plant	✓				Moder... ea...
Forest Lily				▲▲		Depends on the species	Flowering House Plant Bromeliad				*Not good, but will have to stay!*	M...
Vriesea				▲▲▲	—	Height 3 ft Flowers 6–9 in. long	Temporary Pot Plant	Pink	88	Aunt Mary		
Calla Lily				▲		Flowers ½ in. across						

Clover

OXALIS

n. bulb in spring — the leaves ne at the top of 1–2 ft flower

pact hybrids classed as ral rings of petals). Some of **T. kaufmanniana** and er for blooms in January to

SIS
as a change from Hyacinths or onths later the 1 ft flower stalk bular flowers at the top

splendens (Flaming Sword) as the 0 to 2 ft long — bright red above the number of other Vrieseas available, pact ones like **V. minor** and the

A AETHIOPICA
t world. The upturned white trumpets are ve the fleshy, arrow-shaped leaves. The the plant is actively growing

Note down your views on performance. In case of a poor showing check in The House Plant Expert to see if you are doing something wrong. A change of location may be needed

Write in the year when you obtained the plant. Use a pencil tick if you propose to buy the variety

Note plant or bloom details of the unlisted variety if you know them

Write in the name of the supplier — grower, garden centre, DIY store etc. This information is useful if you have cause to complain at a later date. State 'Cutting' or name of friend or relative if applicable

Write in the name of any unlisted variety you are growing or propose to grow in the house or conservatory

FOLIAGE PLANTS

Varieties

	Common name	CONDITIONS REQUIRED			Water:	
		Light	Air humidity	Warmth	Growing period	Resting period
ABUTILON STRIATUM THOMPSONII The Abutilons are generally grown for their blooms — this one is cultivated for its yellow-splashed leaves. Orange flowers in summer are a bonus. Quick-growing — cut back in autumn and repot in spring	Spotted Flowering Maple					
ACALYPHA WILKESIANA This is one for the greenhouse rather than the living room. High humidity and warm nights are needed in winter, so new plants are usually raised from cuttings each year. Coppery colouring fades in poor light	Copper Leaf					
ACORUS GRAMINEUS VARIEGATUS A grassy plant with white-striped leaves borne in fan-like tufts. An easy plant to grow provided you keep the compost wet at all times and place in an unheated room in winter. Unspectacular and uncommon	Sweet Flag					
ADIANTUM The Maidenhair Ferns have wiry stems, delicate leaves and a delicate constitution. **A. raddianum** is the easiest to grow — the arching **A. tenerum farleyense** is perhaps the most attractive. **A. capillus-veneris** is one of the very few British wild flowers grown as a house plant	Maidenhair Fern					
AEONIUM ARBOREUM The fleshy leaves of this succulent are borne in a rosette. Several of these rosettes are carried on the top of branched stems to produce a tree-like plant. Choose the variety **atropurpureum** (purple-brown) or **Schwarzkopf** (near black)	Aeonium					
AGAVE A genus of imposing succulents with long and pointed leaves. **A. americana** is the popular one — there are several varieties with striped leaves. Choose another species where space is limited — there is **A. filifera** covered with fine threads and **A. victoriae-reginae** with its leaves tipped by black spines	Century Plant					
AGLAONEMA The Aglaonemas are popular house plants, grown primarily for their large leaves rather than the unspectacular flowers. All varieties tolerate shade, but the need for light increases with the amount of white or yellow present. **A. modestum** is all-green — **A. Silver Queen** is nearly all-white. The baby is **A. pictum**	Chinese Evergreen					
ALOE Aloes come in all shapes and sizes — there is the diminutive **A. jacunda** with its little cream-blotched leaves and the large **A. ferox** with its 18 in. spiny ones. The popular Aloes are stemless rosettes of 4–6 in. long fleshy leaves. **A. variegata** has white-banded foliage and **A. aristata** has white warts on the leaves	Aloe					
ARAUCARIA HETEROPHYLLA A slow-growing tree bearing stiff branches covered with prickly needle-like leaves. These branches are neatly arranged in tiers giving a Christmas-tree effect. Not difficult, but even with expert care the loss of some lower branches and leaves will occur with age	Norfolk Island Pine					
ASPARAGUS The Asparagus species which have become popular are distinctly fern-like in appearance, bearing fine needle-like leaves. **A. plumosus** has horizontal branchlets on wiry stems — **A. densiflorus sprengeri** bears trailing stems. Less well-known is **A. meyeri** — a green bottle-brush plant. The large-leaved trailing variety called Smilax by florists is **A. asparagoides**. Even larger leaved is **A. falcatus**, with 3 ft stems and 2 in. long strap-like leaves	Asparagus Fern					

ABUTILON STRIATUM THOMPSONII
Spotted Flowering Maple

ACALYPHA WILKESIANA
Copper Leaf

ACORUS GRAMINEUS
Sweet Flag

ADIANTUM RADDIANUM
Maidenhair Fern

AEONIUM ARBOREUM ATROPURPUREUM
Aeonium

Foliage house plants are varieties which are grown for the display provided by their leaves and/or stems or their overall attractive shape. Flowers may appear but these blooms are generally regarded as a minor bonus. Almost all are perennial and evergreen under ordinary room conditions, provided that their requirements are met. These requirements range from undemanding, as in the case of the near-indestructible Aspidistra and Chlorophytum, to extremely fussy if you grow plants like Calathea. Not all foliage house plants are perennial and evergreen — some are short-lived (e.g Coleus) and a few others lose their leaves in the resting season (e.g Caladium). Foliage house plants provide an essential background to any collection. They are attractive all year round, but some of them have to be kept in an unheated room during winter.

PLANT DETAILS		HOUSE PLANT RECORD					Easy or difficult
Dimensions	Family group	Variety grown	Year of arrival	Supplier	Performance during the year		
Height 5ft — Leaves 4 in. long	Evergreen Foliage Plant						Moderately easy
Height 4 ft — Leaves 5 in. long	Evergreen Foliage Plant						Difficult
Leaves 15 in. long	Evergreen Foliage Plant						Easy
Height 1 ft — Leaflets ½ in. long	Evergreen Foliage Plant — Fern						Difficult
Leaves 2–4 in. long	Evergreen Foliage Plant — Succulent						Moderately easy
Leaves 6 in.–4 ft long	Evergreen Foliage Plant — Succulent						Easy
Leaves 6–18 in. long	Evergreen Foliage Plant						Moderately easy
Height 3 in.–10 ft	Evergreen Foliage Plant — Succulent						Easy
Height 5 ft — Leaves ½ in. long	Evergreen Foliage Plant						Easy
Height 1–5 ft	Evergreen Foliage Plant						Easy

VARIETIES

AGAVE AMERICANA
Century Plant

AGLAONEMA MODESTUM
Chinese Evergreen

ALOE ARISTATA
Lace Aloe

ARAUCARIA HETEROPHYLLA
Norfolk Island Pine

ASPARAGUS PLUMOSUS
Asparagus Fern

FOLIAGE PLANTS

Varieties

Common name	CONDITIONS REQUIRED				
	Light	Air humidity	Warmth	Water: Growing period	Water: Resting period

ASPIDISTRA ELATIOR
An old favourite which is making a comeback. The dark green leaves can withstand neglect, draughts and shade — but it is not idiot-proof. It will die if the soil is kept saturated and the leaves are harmed by both sunlight and frequent potting

Common name: Cast Iron Plant — Light: semi-shade curtain; Air humidity: low; Growing: 2 drops; Resting: 1 drop

ASPLENIUM NIDUS
A fern, but you would never guess it from its appearance. The large and shiny leaves surround the fibrous 'nest' at the centre of the plant. An Asplenium which is truly fern-like is **A. bulbiferum** — the finely divided fronds bear tiny plantlets

Common name: Bird's Nest Fern — Light: curtain; Air humidity: high; Growing: 3 drops; Resting: 1 drop

AUCUBA JAPONICA VARIEGATA
This woody shrub is grown for its large yellow-spotted leaves which are borne in profusion. It is useful for rooms which are not heated in winter. Serious leaf fall occurs under hot and dry conditions

Common name: Spotted Laurel — Light: curtain; Air humidity: medium; Growing: 3 drops; Resting: 2 drops

BEAUCARNEA RECURVATA
A shaggy-looking false palm with 3–5 ft long narrow leaves and a swollen bulb-like base. A rarity in Britain, but useful if you want a tall specimen plant that needs little attention

Common name: Pony Tail Plant — Light: sun/curtain; Air humidity: low; Growing: 2 drops; Resting: 1 drop

BEGONIA
Included here are the Begonias grown solely or mainly for their foliage. This group is dominated by **B. rex**. The leaves are large and lop-sided with a bewildering range of colours amongst the named varieties. Rather similar is **B. masoniana**, grown for its Iron Cross pattern on its puckered leaves. There are several tall-growing species, such as **B. maculata** (white-spotted leaves) and **B. metallica** (purple-veined 'metallic' leaves). Where space is limited choose the compact **B. boweri** (6–9 in.) or its hybrid **B. Tiger**. **B. Cleopatra** is a small bronzy-leaved plant

Common name: Begonia — Light: curtain; Air humidity: medium; Growing: 2 drops; Resting: 1 drop

BLECHNUM GIBBUM
Choose this one if you want to grow a miniature tree fern — the mature plant has a 3 ft trunk. The palm-like crown is made up of large stiff fronds, each frond being divided into wavy leaflets. A smaller relative is **B. braziliense**

Common name: Blechnum — Light: curtain; Air humidity: medium; Growing: 3 drops; Resting: 2 drops

BREYNIA NIVOSA ROSEOPICTA
The pink, white and green variegated leaves have a flower-like appearance — hence the common name. It was introduced as a house plant during the 1980s. Basically a conservatory plant, it will produce a small bush in the home if the air is kept sufficiently moist

Common name: Leaf Flower — Light: curtain; Air humidity: high; Growing: 3 drops; Resting: 1 drop

BRYOPHYLLUM DAIGREMONTIANUM
The Bryophyllums belong to the small group of plants which bear plantlets on their leaves. The most popular one is the Devil's Backbone, sometimes sold as **Kalanchoe daigremontiana**. It is an erect and unbranched plant with triangular saw-edged leaves

Common name: Devil's Backbone — Light: sun; Air humidity: low; Growing: 3 drops; Resting: 1 drop

BUXUS
Box is a favourite shrub outdoors, but it has only recently been accepted as a house plant. **B. sempervirens** (Common Box) can be grown, but the Small-leaved Box (**B. microphylla**) is a better choice. Prune to keep in shape

Common name: Box — Light: sun/curtain; Air humidity: medium; Growing: 3 drops; Resting: 2 drops

CALADIUM
The striking arrow-shaped leaves are spectacular — paper-thin and beautifully marked in attractive colours. Long stalks bear these foot-long leaves above the pots. This foliage is not permanent — it lasts from late spring to early autumn

Common name: Caladium — Light: curtain; Air humidity: high; Growing: 2 drops; Resting: 1 drop

CALATHEA
The showiest Calathea is undoubtedly **C. makoyana** — the Peacock Plant. The pale green 1 ft long leaves bear a tracery of dark green lines and blotches. The pink-striped leaves of **C. ornata** are smaller. **C. insignis** has lance-shaped leaves

Common name: Calathea — Light: curtain; Air humidity: high; Growing: 3 drops; Resting: 2 drops

CALLISIA ELEGANS
C. elegans (sometimes sold as **Setcreasea striata**) has Tradescantia-like leaves and long creeping stems. The upper surface is dull and boldly striped with white lines. **C. fragrans** is an erect plant — the leaves turn pink in bright light

Common name: Striped Inch Plant — Light: curtain; Air humidity: medium; Growing: 3 drops; Resting: 1 drop

CAREX MORROWII VARIEGATA
This grassy plant is not often seen but it is extremely easy to look after indoors. Its arching white-striped leaves make it a useful item for a terrarium or indoor garden. It is one of the most durable of all house plants

Common name: Japanese Sedge — Light: curtain; Air humidity: low; Growing: 2 drops; Resting: 2 drops

ASPIDISTRA ELATIOR
Cast Iron Plant

ASPLENIUM NIDUS
Bird's Nest Fern

AUCUBA JAPONICA VARIEGATA
Spotted Laurel

BEGONIA REX
Rex Begonia

PLANT DETAILS		HOUSE PLANT RECORD					Easy or difficult
Dimensions	Family group	Variety grown	Year of arrival	Supplier	Performance during the year		
Leaves 1½ ft long	Evergreen Foliage Plant						Easy
Leaves 2 ft long	Evergreen Foliage Plant — Fern						Moderately easy
Height 5 ft	Evergreen Foliage Plant						Easy
Height 6 ft	Evergreen Foliage Plant						Easy
Height 6 in.–6 ft	Evergreen Foliage Plant						Moderately easy
Leaves 3 ft long	Evergreen Foliage Plant — Fern						Moderately easy
Height 1 ft	Evergreen Foliage Plant						Moderately difficult
Height 2 ft — Leaves 4 in. long	Evergreen Foliage Plant — Succulent						Easy
Height 4 ft	Evergreen Foliage Plant						Easy
Leaves 1 ft long	Deciduous Foliage Plant						Difficult
Height 1–2 ft — Leaves 6–18 in. long	Evergreen Foliage Plant — Maranta Group						Difficult
Leaves 1–1½ in. long	Evergreen Foliage Plant — Tradescantia Group						Easy
Leaves 1 ft long	Evergreen Foliage Plant						Easy

VARIETIES

BLECHNUM GIBBUM
Blechnum

BRYOPHYLLUM DAIGREMONTIANUM
Devil's Backbone

BUXUS SEMPERVIRENS
Common Box

CALADIUM HORTULANUM
Angel's Wings

CALATHEA MAKOYANA
Peacock Plant

Varieties

FOLIAGE PLANTS

CONDITIONS REQUIRED

	Common name	Light	Air humidity	Warmth	Water: Growing period	Water: Resting period
CARYOTA MITIS The Fishtail Palms get their name from the shape of the leaflets, which are about 6 in. long and 4 in. wide. **C. mitis** is the favourite one — lots of ragged-edged leaflets on arching fronds. **C. urens** is larger but less attractive	Fishtail Palm					
CEROPEGIA WOODII An unusual succulent for a hanging basket or a pot standing on a shelf. The wiry stems bear heart-shaped fleshy leaves which are dark green blotched with silver. Unfortunately the foliage is rather sparse	Rosary Vine					
CHAMAEDOREA Two Chamaedoreas are offered for sale — the narrow-leaved **C. seifrizii** and the broad-leaved **C. erumpens**. They are popular with interior decorators in the U.S. — tall cane-like stems are produced	Reed Palm					
CHAMAEROPS HUMILIS There are several Fan Palms — the family feature is the large frond (leaf) which is divided into a number of leaflets radiating from the base. The easiest to grow is **C. humilis** — **C. excelsa** (Windmill Palm) is difficult	European Fan Palm					
CHLOROPHYTUM COMOSUM One of the most popular house plants and an ideal one for beginners. It will grow in hot or cold rooms, sunny windows or shady corners and it doesn't mind dry air. The leaves arch attractively, and plantlets are borne on wiry stems	Spider Plant					
CHRYSALIDOCARPUS LUTESCENS Yellowish-green leaflets are borne on the top of cane-like stems — a fine choice if you want a bold focal point. It is sometimes sold as **Areca lutescens** — more popular in the U.S. than in Britain	Areca Palm					
CISSUS ANTARCTICA A great favourite for covering screens and other large areas. The quick-growing stems cling to the supports by means of tendrils, clothing the uprights with their leathery leaves. Useful for hanging baskets	Kangaroo Vine					
CISSUS DISCOLOR A delicate vine needing warmth and high humidity around the foliage. Each leaf is blotched with silver and purple — the underside is red. Pinch out stem tips to induce bushy growth	Begonia Vine					
COCOS The true Coconut Palm (**C. nucifera**) is sometimes offered for sale, but it is short-lived indoors. Its near relative **C. weddeliana** (Dwarf Coconut Palm) is more satisfactory as a house plant. An attractive palm — the leaflets are very narrow. It needs warmth and high humidity	Coconut Palm					
CODIAEUM VARIEGATUM PICTUM Vivid colours and varied leaf shapes make the Crotons a popular choice, but they are not easy to grow. They hate cold winter nights, draughts, sudden changes in temperature and periods of dryness at the roots. Scores of varieties are available — examples are **Vulcan**, **Reidii**, **Mrs Iceton**, **Bravo** and **Appleleaf**	Croton					
COFFEA ARABICA The Coffee Tree can be grown indoors and the shrub may even flower after a few years. The variety **nana** is smaller but it flowers more readily. Leaves are shiny and wavy-edged. Not difficult, but avoid draughts	Coffee Tree					
COLEUS BLUMEI Plants are easily raised from seed or by taking cuttings — the cheapest way to provide brightly-coloured foliage for a house plant collection. Care is not difficult — raise new plants each year. There are many named varieties — examples are **Sabre Mixed**, **Volcano**, **Firebird** and the dwarf **Sabre**	Flame Nettle					
CORDYLINE AUSTRALIS The easiest Cordyline to grow — a false palm with a stout trunk and a crown of narrow arching leaves. A useful specimen plant which does not need warm conditions — it can be kept outdoors in summer	Cabbage Tree					

CARYOTA MITIS
Fishtail Palm

CEROPEGIA WOODII
Rosary Vine

CHAMAEDOREA SEIFRIZII
Reed Palm

CHLOROPHYTUM COMOSUM
Spider Plant

CHRYSALIDOCARPUS LUTESCENS
Areca Palm

CISSUS ANTARCTICA
Kangaroo Vine

PLANT DETAILS		HOUSE PLANT RECORD					Easy or difficult
Dimensions	Family group	Variety grown	Year of arrival	Supplier	Performance during the year		
Height 6–8 ft	Evergreen Foliage Plant — Palm						Moderately easy
Height 3 ft Leaves ¾ in. long	Evergreen Foliage Plant — Succulent						Easy
Height 6–10 ft	Evergreen Foliage Plant — Palm						Moderately easy
Height 3 ft	Evergreen Foliage Plant — Palm						Moderately easy
Leaves 9 in. long	Evergreen Foliage Plant						Easy
Height 4 ft	Evergreen Foliage Plant — Palm						Moderately easy
Height 10 ft Leaves 4 in. long	Evergreen Foliage Plant — Vine						Easy
Leaves 6 in. long	Evergreen Foliage Plant — Vine						Difficult
Height 6 ft Leaves 2 ft long	Evergreen Foliage Plant — Palm						Difficult
Height 1–4 ft	Evergreen Foliage Plant						Moderately difficult
Height 4 ft Leaves 6 in. long	Evergreen Foliage Plant						Moderately easy
Height 1–2 ft	Temporary Foliage Plant						Moderately easy
Height 3–4 ft	Evergreen Foliage Plant — Dracaena Group						Easy

VARIETIES

COCOS WEDDELIANA
Dwarf Coconut Palm

CODIAEUM VARIEGATUM PICTUM
Croton

COFFEA ARABICA
Coffee Tree

COLEUS BLUMEI
Flame Nettle

CORDYLINE AUSTRALIS
Cabbage Tree

Varieties

FOLIAGE PLANTS

	Common name	CONDITIONS REQUIRED				
		Light	Air humidity	Warmth	Water: Growing period	Water: Resting period
CORDYLINE TERMINALIS This compact false palm is sold under many names — **Dracaena terminalis**, **Ti Plant**, **Red Dracaena** etc. The leaves are usually splashed with red — **Rededge** is the favourite variety. Others include **Atom** and **Kiwi**	Ti Plant	semi-shade	◑	warm	💧💧💧	💧💧
COTYLEDON The best known Cotyledon is **C. undulata** (Silver Crown) — a shrubby succulent bearing wavy-edged and bloom-covered leaves. **C. orbiculata** is larger with red-edged leaves	Cotyledon	sun	○	warm	💧💧💧	💧
CRASSULA There are no typical foliage or growth characteristics to help you identify a plant as a Crassula. Leaves range from scale-like to several inches long. The most popular species is **C. argentea** (Jade Plant) — shiny red-edged leaves are 1–2 in. long. **C. arborescens** is rather similar, but **C. lycopodioides** has tiny fleshy leaves and **C. perforata** has paired leaves surrounding the stem	Crassula	semi-shade	○	warm	💧💧💧	💧
CRYPTANTHUS These low-growing plants are best kept in a glass container. The leaves are wavy-edged and colourful. There is a wide range to choose from — plain, striped and banded in green, red, brown and yellow. The largest is **C. fosterianus**. The most difficult is **C. bromelioides**	Earth Star	semi-shade	◌	hot	💧💧	💧💧
CTENANTHE OPPENHEIMIANA TRICOLOR An eye-catching member of the Maranta family — the velvety leaves bear cream-coloured blotches. This plant has many hates, such as direct sunlight, cold and hard water and temperatures below 60°F	Never Never Plant	shade	◑	hot	💧💧	💧
CYANOTIS KEWENSIS Similar to the closely-related Tradescantia but it bears hairy leaves and is a little more difficult to grow. The underside of the fleshy leaves is purple — a useful plant for hanging baskets	Teddy Bear Vine	semi-shade	◌	warm	💧💧	💧💧
CYCAS REVOLUTA Palm-like, but unrelated to the true palms. An extremely slow-growing plant, producing just one leaf per year from the ball-like base. The foliage is stiff and arching	Sago Palm	shade	◑	warm	💧💧	💧
CYPERUS The popular ones are **C. diffusus** (1–2 ft) and **C. alternifolius** (3–4 ft). Thin stems are topped by radiating strap-like leaves. There is just one golden rule — keep the roots constantly wet	Umbrella Plant	semi-shade	◌	warm	💧💧💧	💧💧💧
CYRTOMIUM FALCATUM Cyrtomium is an excellent fern to buy — it can withstand dry air and draughts. **C. falcatum** (Fishtail Fern) has smooth-edged leaflets — the variety **rochfordianum** (Holly Fern) has saw-edged leaflets	Cyrtomium	shade	◌	warm	💧💧	💧💧
DAVALLIA CANARIENSIS Davallia is grown for its thick and hairy rhizomes which grow over the side of the pot. The triangular fronds are made up of tiny leaflets on wiry stalks. It grows in drier air than most other ferns	Hare's Foot Fern	shade	◌	warm	💧💧	💧💧
DIEFFENBACHIA A much loved tree-like plant with large leaves. The popular species is **D. picta** and the varieties range from all-green to practically all-cream. The leaves are about 10 in. long — attractive varieties include **Exotica** and **Marianne**. **D. amoena** is larger (18 in. leaves) and has cream-striped foliage — **Tropic Snow** is striking	Dumb Cane	shade	◑	hot	💧💧	💧
DIZYGOTHECA ELEGANTISSIMA A graceful plant with leaves divided into finger-like serrated leaflets which are almost black. Unfortunately its constitution is as delicate as its appearance — it hates dry air, wet compost and sudden changes in temperature	False Aralia	shade	◑	hot	💧💧	💧
DRACAENA Most Dracaenas are false palms — the leafless woody trunk bears a crown of long leaves. Some are easy to grow, such as **D. marginata** and **D. draco** (Dragon Tree). Others need moist air — popular ones include the yellow-striped **D. fragrans** and the white-striped **D. deremensis warneckii**. The baby of the group is the Ribbon Plant (**D. sanderana**) — white-edged leaves, height 2 ft. Not all are palm-like — **D. godseffiana** is an easy-to-grow shrub with cream-spotted leaves	Dracaena	shade	◑	warm	💧💧💧	💧💧

CORDYLINE TERMINALIS
Ti Plant

COTYLEDON UNDULATA
Silver Crown

CRASSULA ARGENTEA
Jade Plant

CYANOTIS KEWENSIS
Teddy Bear Vine

CYCAS REVOLUTA
Sago Palm

PLANT DETAILS		HOUSE PLANT RECORD				Easy or difficult
Dimensions	Family group	Variety grown	Year of arrival	Supplier	Performance during the year	
Height 1–2 ft — Leaves 9 in. long	Evergreen Foliage Plant — Dracaena Group					Moderately easy
Height 1–2 ft	Evergreen Foliage Plant — Succulent					Moderately easy
Depends on the species	Evergreen Foliage Plant — Succulent					Moderately easy
Leaves 4–15 in. long	Evergreen Foliage Plant — Bromeliad					Moderately difficult
Leaves 1½ ft long	Evergreen Foliage Plant — Maranta Group					Difficult
Leaves 1 in. long	Evergreen Foliage Plant — Tradescantia Group					Moderately easy
Height 2 ft	Evergreen Foliage Plant					Moderately easy
Height 1–4 ft	Evergreen Foliage Plant					Easy
Leaves 2 ft long	Evergreen Foliage Plant — Fern					Easy
Leaves 1 ft long	Evergreen Foliage Plant — Fern					Moderately easy
Leaves 9–18 in. long	Evergreen Foliage Plant					Moderately difficult
Height 5 ft — Leaves 6 in. long	Evergreen Foliage Plant					Difficult
Leaves 1½–2 ft long	Evergreen Foliage Plant					Depends on the species

CYPERUS DIFFUSUS Umbrella Plant

CYRTOMIUM FALCATUM Fishtail Fern

DIEFFENBACHIA OERSTEDII Dumb Cane

DIZYGOTHECA ELEGANTISSIMA False Aralia

DRACAENA SANDERANA Ribbon Plant

Varieties

FOLIAGE PLANTS

Common name	CONDITIONS REQUIRED				
	Light	Air humidity	Warmth	Water: Growing period	Water: Resting period

ECHEVERIA
Some Echeverias grow as rosette-topped trees — **E. harmsii** is an example. Others grow as flattened rosettes — the leaves are 1–3 in. long and each species has its own distinctive feature

Common name	Light	Air humidity	Warmth	Growing period	Resting period
Echeveria	full sun	open circle	thermometer	2 drops	1 drop

EUPHORBIA
A few Euphorbias are grown for their stems rather than their flowers. There is the cactus-like **E. grandicornis**, the globular **E. obesa** and the pencil-stemmed **E. tirucalli** (Milk Bush)

Euphorbia	full sun	open circle	thermometer	2 drops	1 drop

FATSHEDERA LIZEI
This easy-to-grow hybrid of Fatsia and Hedera deserves its popularity. Support is needed, or you can pinch out the tips and grow it as a bush. **Variegata** is the white-blotched form

Ivy Tree	filtered	dotted circle	thermometer	3 drops	1 drop

FATSIA JAPONICA
An old favourite with deeply-lobed leaves and a tough constitution — it makes an excellent specimen plant. There are several varieties, including **variegata** (cream-edged foliage) and **moseri** (compact growth habit)

Castor Oil Plant	filtered	dotted circle	thermometer	3 drops	1 drop

FAUCARIA TIGRINA
The fleshy leaves bear "teeth". These tooth-like spines along the edges of the leaf are quite soft and so the plant is not as vicious as it looks. Yellow flowers appear in summer

Tiger Jaws	full sun	open circle	thermometer	3 drops	1 drop

FICUS
This family contains house plants which vary from stately trees to lowly creepers. The unchallenged head of the family is the Rubber Plant (**F. elastica decora** or **F. elastica robusta**). The Weeping Fig (**F. benjamina**) is increasing in popularity. The giant of the tree-like group is **F. lyrata** with 18 in. long leaves. At the other end of the scale are two trailing types. **F. pumila** has 1 in. long heart-shaped leaves — **F. radicans variegata** has larger (3 in.) cream-edged leaves

Fig	filtered	dotted circle	thermometer	2 drops	1 drop

FITTONIA
Fittonia is easily recognised — the leaves bear a network of veins. The large-leaved **F. verschaffeltii** has deep pink veins — the white-veined **F. argyroneura** is even more distinctive. Easier to grow is the dwarf **F. argyroneura nana**

Snakeskin Plant	filtered	filled circle	thermometer (high)	3 drops	1 drop

GREVILLEA ROBUSTA
Grevillea is a tall-growing tree with a delicate appearance and ferny foliage. It grows quickly, reaching 6–8 ft in a few years. The lacy effect of the leaves disappears with age

Silk Oak	half sun	dotted circle	thermometer	3 drops	1 drop

GYNURA SARMENTOSA
A popular climber or trailer for a well-lit spot. The foliage has a velvety look — gleaming purple in sunlight. Small, evil-smelling yellow flowers appear in spring. **G. aurantiaca** has larger leaves

Velvet Plant	half sun	dotted circle	thermometer	3 drops	1 drop

HAWORTHIA
Haworthias are low-growing rosettes of thick and warty leaves. **H. margaritifera** is typical — in **H. fasciata** and **H. attenuata** the white warts are arranged in horizontal bands. One species (**H. reinwardtii**) bears erect stems

Haworthia	full sun	open circle	thermometer	2 drops	1 drop

HEDERA
Nearly all of the True Ivies are varieties of the Common or English Ivy (**H. helix**) which bears characteristically lobed leaves. These varieties range in leaf form from simple shields (**scutifolia**) to long-pointed stars (**sagittaefolia**). Edges are smooth or ruffled, and colours vary from simple green (e.g **Chicago**) to mixtures with white (e.g **Harald**), cream (e.g **Glacier**) or yellow (e.g **Jubilee**). The largest-leaved Ivy is **Hedera canariensis Gloire de Marengo** (Canary Island Ivy)

Ivy	filtered	filled circle	thermometer	2 drops	2 drops

HELXINE SOLEIROLII
A dense mass of tiny green leaves — Helxine is excellent in hanging baskets or for covering the soil around tall plants. Easily propagated — simply place a clump on the surface of moist compost

Mind Your Own Business	filtered	dotted circle	thermometer	2 drops	2 drops

HEPTAPLEURUM ARBORICOLA
A quick-growing tree-like plant with about ten leaflets radiating from each leaf stalk. Quite adaptable, but moist air, good light and winter warmth are needed. Variegated forms are available

Parasol Plant	half sun	filled circle (light)	thermometer (high)	3 drops	1 drop

ECHEVERIA HARMSII
Red Echeveria

EUPHORBIA TIRUCALLI
Milk Bush

FATSHEDERA LIZEI
Ivy Tree

FATSIA JAPONICA
Castor Oil Plant

FAUCARIA TIGRINA
Tiger Jaws

PLANT DETAILS		HOUSE PLANT RECORD					Easy or difficult
Dimensions	**Family group**	**Variety grown**	**Year of arrival**	**Supplier**	**Performance during the year**		
Depends on the species	Evergreen Foliage Plant — Succulent						Easy
Depends on the species	Evergreen Foliage Plant — Succulent						Easy
Height 6 ft — Leaves 7 in. long	Evergreen Foliage Plant						Easy
Height 4 ft — Leaves 1 ft long	Evergreen Foliage Plant						Easy
Leaves 2 in. long	Evergreen Foliage Plant — Succulent						Moderately easy
Depends on the species	Evergreen Foliage Plant						Moderately easy
Leaves 1–2 in. long	Evergreen Foliage Plant						Difficult
Height 8 ft	Evergreen Foliage Plant						Easy
Leaves 3 in. long	Evergreen Foliage Plant						Moderately easy
Leaves 2–3 in. long	Evergreen Foliage Plant — Succulent						Easy
Leaves 1–4 in. long	Evergreen Foliage Plant						Moderately easy
$\frac{1}{5}$ Leaves in. long	Evergreen Foliage Plant						Easy
Height 6 ft	Evergreen Foliage Plant						Moderately easy

VARIETIES

FICUS ELASTICA DECORA
Rubber Plant

FICUS BENJAMINA
Weeping Fig

FITTONIA ARGYRONEURA NANA
Snakeskin Plant

GREVILLEA ROBUSTA
Silk Oak

HEDERA HELIX
Ivy

Varieties

FOLIAGE PLANTS

	Common name	CONDITIONS REQUIRED				
		Light	Air humidity	Warmth	Water: Growing period	Water: Resting period
HOWEA These are the popular Palm Court plants — **H. forsteriana (Kentia forsteriana)** is the British favourite and **H. belmoreana** is the one found in the U.S. It is not easy to distinguish between them	Kentia Palm	shade	medium humidity	warm	●●●	●
HYPOESTES SANGUINOLENTA In a well-lit spot the oval leaves are covered with pink spots and patches — Polka Dot Plant is an alternative common name. **Splash** is the brightest variety. Pinch out tips occasionally	Freckle Face	semi-shade	medium humidity	warm	●●	●
IRESINE The red Iresine is Bloodleaf (**I. herbstii**) — more popular in the U.S. than in Britain. More colourful is the variety **aureoreticulata**, known as Chicken Gizzard. Stems are red, leaves are green and veins a bright yellow	Iresine	sun	moist	warm	●●●	●
KALANCHOE TOMENTOSA Panda Plant is the most popular of the foliage Kalanchoes. The brown-edged fleshy leaves have a furry surface. Other Kalanchoes include **K. marmorata** (Pen Wiper) which bears brown-blotched leaves	Panda Plant	sun	dry	warm	●	●
KLEINIA ARTICULATA This succulent is grown for its swollen bloom-coated stems — the leaves appear in winter but soon fall. Pale yellow flowers open in summer. You may find this plant listed as **Senecio articulatus**	Candle Plant	sun	dry	cool	●●	●●
LITHOPS Living Stones mimic the pebbles which abound in their natural habitat. Two thick leaves are fused to produce a squat stone-like body. Most belong to the genus **Lithops** — numerous species are available. Daisy-like flowers appear in autumn	Living Stones	sun	dry	warm	●	●
LIVISTONA CHINENSIS Like Chamaerops, this is a relatively easy palm to grow. The large fronds (leaves) are partly divided into leaflets to give a fan-like appearance. The features here are toothed leaf stalks and leaflets which droop at the tips	Chinese Fan Palm	semi-shade	moist	warm	●●	●
MARANTA The common name comes from the unusual habit of folding and raising the foliage at night. All the popular varieties belong to the species **M. leuconeura**. For prominent red veins buy the variety **erythrophylla** (sold as **M. tricolor**). Another red-veined one is **Fascinator**. For white veins pick **massangeana** and for brown patches on bright green leaves the usual choice is **kerchoveana**	Prayer Plant	shade	medium humidity	warm	●●●	●
MIKANIA TERNATA A quick-growing trailing plant which was introduced a few years ago. The leaves have a distinctly red or purple sheen — the veins and underside are purple. Mist with care — do not wet leaves	Plush Vine	semi-shade	moist	warm	●●	●
MIMOSA PUDICA A branching plant with delicate spiny branches bearing feathery leaves. The leaves fold and the branches droop when touched — hence the common name. Ball-like pink flowers appear in summer	Sensitive Plant	semi-shade	medium humidity	cool	●●	●
MONSTERA DELICIOSA A favourite for many years. Provide stout support and a large and impressive plant is soon obtained — the leaves will be perforated and deeply cut if winter brightness is provided. Push aerial roots into the compost. If space is limited grow the dwarf variety **borsigiana**	Swiss Cheese Plant	shade	medium humidity	warm	●	●
NEANTHE BELLA The most widely grown of all indoor palms. The dwarf nature of Neanthe makes it ideal for small rooms and bottle gardens. After a few years it will reach its adult height and tiny yellow flowers and small fruit appear. Sometimes sold as **Chamaedorea elegans**	Parlour Palm	shade	medium humidity	warm	●●●	●
NEPHROLEPIS EXALTATA BOSTONIENSIS If you can grow only one fern, choose this one. It is not difficult and the long graceful fronds arch downwards. Leaflets are arranged along the midrib in herringbone fashion — these leaflets may be large (e.g **rooseveltii**) or small (e.g **maassii**). In some varieties they are further divided to give a feathery effect (e.g **Fluffy Ruffles**)	Boston Fern	shade	moist	warm	●●●	●●

HOWEA FORSTERIANA
Kentia Palm

HYPOESTES SANGUINOLENTA
Freckle Face

IRESINE HERBSTII
Bloodleaf

KALANCHOE TOMENTOSA
Panda Plant

KLEINIA ARTICULATA
Candle Plant

PLANT DETAILS		HOUSE PLANT RECORD					Easy or difficult
Dimensions	**Family group**	**Variety grown**	**Year of arrival**	**Supplier**	**Performance during the year**		
Height 8 ft	Evergreen Foliage Plant — Palm						Easy
Height 2 ft — Leaves 2 in. long	Evergreen Foliage Plant						Moderately easy
Height 1½ ft — Leaves 3 in. long	Evergreen Foliage Plant						Moderately difficult
Height 1½ ft — Leaves 2 in. long	Evergreen Foliage Plant — Succulent						Easy
Height 2 ft	Evergreen Foliage Plant — Succulent						Moderately easy
Height ½–2 in.	Evergreen Foliage Plant — Succulent						Easy
Leaves 3 ft long	Evergreen Foliage Plant — Palm						Moderately easy
Height 9–12 in. — Leaves 6 in. long	Evergreen Foliage Plant — Maranta Group						Moderately difficult
Height 7 ft — Leaflets 2 in. long	Evergreen Foliage Plant						Moderately difficult
Height 2 ft	Evergreen Foliage Plant						Moderately easy
Height up to 20 ft — Leaves 1½ ft long	Evergreen Foliage Plant						Easy
Height 3 ft	Evergreen Foliage Plant — Palm						Easy
Leaves 1½–2 ft long	Evergreen Foliage Plant — Fern						Moderately easy

VARIETIES

MARANTA LEUCONEURA KERCHOVEANA
Prayer Plant

MIMOSA PUDICA
Sensitive Plant

MONSTERA DELICIOSA
Swiss Cheese Plant

NEANTHE BELLA
Parlour Palm

NEPHROLEPIS EXALTATA BOSTONIENSIS
Boston Fern

FOLIAGE PLANTS

Varieties

Description	Common name	Light	Air humidity	Warmth	Water: Growing period	Water: Resting period
OPHIOPOGON JABURAN An undemanding grass-like plant for an unheated room. Green-and-white striped varieties are available, and in summer there are small clusters of white drooping flowers. Dwarf Lily Turf (**O. japonicus**) has blackish green leaves	White Lily Turf	▨	◉	🌡	💧💧💧	💧
OPLISMENUS HIRTELLUS An excellent alternative to Tradescantia for hanging baskets and wall pots. Discard old plants and take cuttings each spring to maintain the display. Choose **variegatus** for white-, pink- and green-striped leaves	Basket Grass	▨	◉	🌡	💧💧💧	💧
PACHYPHYTUM OVIFERUM A small and popular succulent — the tips of the short stems are crowded with sugar almond-shaped leaves. The surface of the leaves is covered with a silvery-white bloom	Sugar Almond Plant	☀	○	🌡	💧💧	💧
PANDANUS VEITCHII The long arching leaves are spirally arranged around the stem — they are striped in cream or yellow. Take care — the spines at the edges of the leaves are sharp. Keep compost almost dry in winter	Screw Pine	▨	◉	🌡	💧💧💧	💧
PEDILANTHUS TITHYMALOIDES **P. tithymaloides** is unmistakable — the fleshy stems zig-zag sharply. The variety **variegatus** is the popular one — oval, waxy leaves edged with white and pink. The milky sap is an irritant — so take care	Jacob's Ladder	☀	○	🌡	💧	💧
PELARGONIUM The flowering Geraniums are the popular ones, but there is a small group which are grown for their leaves which are aromatic when crushed. Choose **graveolens** (rose), **crispum** (lemon), **tomentosum** (mint) or **odoratissimum** (apple)	Scented-leaved Geranium	◑	○	🌡	💧💧💧	💧
PELLAEA Pellaea has an unusual feature for a fern — it prefers dry surroundings rather than the moist air required by most ferns. **P. rotundifolia** (Button Fern) has ½ in. round leaflets along the arching fronds. **P. viridis** (Green Brake Fern) has tiny leaflets and is much more fern-like	Pellaea	▨	○	🌡	💧💧💧	💧
PELLIONIA There are two species — **P. daveauana** (Watermelon Pellionia) and **P. pulchra** (Satin Pellionia). These oval-leaved trailers are useful in a terrarium but are rather too delicate for hanging basket use	Pellionia	▨	●	🌡	💧💧💧	💧
PEPEROMIA Slow growing and compact plants which are widely used in bottle gardens and other situations where space is limited. There are scores of types — some produce 'rat-tail' flower spikes. Four are popular. **P. scandens variegata** is a climber/trailer with yellow-edged waxy leaves. The 4–6 in. high bushy **P. caperata** with corrugated leaves is more familiar — so is the metallic-leaved **P. hederaefolia**. Commonest of all, perhaps, is the fleshy-leaved, yellow-edged **P. magnoliaefolia**	Peperomia	▨	◉	🌡	💧💧	💧
PHILODENDRON The Philodendrons are an extremely important group of house plants — the large-leaved ones are widely used by interior designers. There are two basic types — the first type, the climbers, are suitable for the average room. **P. scandens** (Sweetheart Plant) is the smallest, easiest and the most popular. The leaves are heart-shaped and shiny. Others include **P. panduriforme** (fiddle-shaped leaves) and **P. melanochrysum** (velvety leaves). Most of the second type, the non-climbers, produce immense, deeply-lobed leaves. Both **P. selloum** and **P. bipinnatifidum** need a lot of space	Philodendron	▨	◉	🌡	💧💧💧	💧
PHOENIX The True Date Palm (**P. dactylifera**) is less attractive but quicker growing than the species sold as house plants — **P. canariensis** (6 ft — Canary Date Palm) and **P. roebelenii** (3 ft — Pygmy Date Palm). Fronds bear very narrow leaflets	Date Palm	▨	◉	🌡	💧💧💧	💧
PHYLLITIS SCOLOPENDRIUM This fern bears long, spear-shaped leaves — wavy-edged and borne on dark brown stems. The varieties **crispum** and **undulatum** have frilly margins. This is a hardy plant which needs cool conditions in winter	Hart's Tongue Fern	▨	◉	🌡	💧💧💧	💧

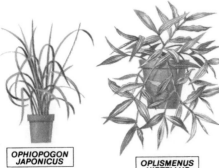

OPHIOPOGON JAPONICUS
Dwarf Lily Turf

OPLISMENUS HIRTELLUS
Basket Grass

PACHYPHYTUM OVIFERUM
Sugar Almond Plant

PANDANUS VEITCHII
Screw Pine

PELLAEA VIRIDIS
Green Brake Fern

PLANT DETAILS		HOUSE PLANT RECORD					Easy or difficult
Dimensions	Family group	Variety grown	Year of arrival	Supplier	Performance during the year		
Leaves 2 ft long	Evergreen Foliage Plant						Moderately easy
Height 3 ft — Leaves 3 in. long	Temporary Foliage Plant						Easy
Height 5 in. — Leaves 1 in. long	Evergreen Foliage Plant — Succulent						Easy
Height 5 ft — Leaves 2–3 ft long	Evergreen Foliage Plant						Moderately difficult
Height 2 ft — Leaves 3 in. long	Evergreen Foliage Plant — Succulent						Moderately easy
Height 2–3 ft — Leaves 1–5 in. long	Evergreen Foliage Plant						Easy
Depends on the species	Evergreen Foliage Plant — Fern						Easy
Depends on the species	Evergreen Foliage Plant						Difficult
Depends on the species	Evergreen Foliage Plant						Moderately easy
Depends on the species	Evergreen Foliage Plant						Moderately easy
Height 3–6 ft	Evergreen Foliage Plant — Palm						Moderately easy
Leaves 1 ft long	Evergreen Foliage Plant — Fern						Moderately easy

VARIETIES

PELLIONIA DAVEAUANA
Watermelon Pellionia

PEPEROMIA CAPERATA
Peperomia

PHILODENDRON SCANDENS
Sweetheart Plant

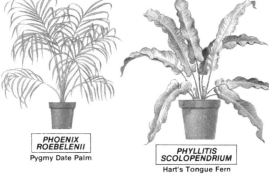

PHOENIX ROEBELENII
Pygmy Date Palm

PHYLLITIS SCOLOPENDRIUM
Hart's Tongue Fern

FOLIAGE PLANTS

Varieties

		CONDITIONS REQUIRED				
Common name		Light	Air humidity	Warmth	Water: Growing period	Resting period

PILEA
A wide variety of bushy and trailing types are available — all are quite easy to grow. There are several small-leaved types, including **P. nummulariifolia** (Creeping Charlie) and **P. microphylla** (Artillery Plant). The most popular Pilea is **P. cadierei** (Aluminium Plant) with silver-blotched and quilted leaves. Other types with 1–3 in. leaves include the bronzy-leaved **P. Norfolk** and **P. repens** and the deeply quilted **P. Moon Valley**
Common name: Pilea

PIPER CROCATUM
The waxy leaves of this trailer/climber are colourful. The puckered surface is dappled with white and veined in dark red. The underside is also red. More eye-catching than Philodendron scandens, but more difficult to find
Common name: Ornamental Pepper

PLATYCERIUM BIFURCATUM
The Staghorn Fern bears large and spectacular fertile fronds (leaves) — greyish-green, spreading and divided at the ends into antler-like lobes. The sterile fronds are smaller, flat and kidney-shaped
Common name: Staghorn Fern

PLECTRANTHUS
These creeping plants are not well-known in Britain, but they flourish in dry air where True Ivies would fail. There is the added bonus of occasional flowers. The foliage of the most popular type (**P. oertendahlii**) bears prominent white veins
Common name: Swedish Ivy

PLEOMELE REFLEXA VARIEGATA
A colourful false palm — the leaves are prominently edged with a bright yellow band. This is not an easy plant to grow — it will fail if the air is dry. Canes are needed to support the weak stems
Common name: Song of India

PODOCARPUS MACROPHYLLUS
Highly durable — an excellent choice for a draughty hall. This indoor tree bears narrow and glossy leaves and can be kept in check by regular pruning. **Maki** is a compact variety
Common name: Buddhist Pine

POLYPODIUM AUREUM
Deeply-cut fronds (leaves) are borne on 1½ ft stalks. The thick rhizome creeps along the surface and this fern tolerates dry air. Sometimes sold as **Phlebodium aureum** — choose the variety **mandaianum**
Common name: Hare's Foot Fern

POLYSCIAS
Attractive oriental trees with twisted stems and decorative foliage. **P. balfouriana** (Dinner Plate Aralia) has round 3 in. leaves — **P. fruticosa** (Ming Aralia) has 8 in. long feathery leaves. Not easy — readily drops its leaves if conditions are not right
Common name: Polyscias

POLYSTICHUM TSUS-SIMENSE
A small plant with upright pointed fronds bearing feathery leaflets. A good fern for beginners, as it is hardy and does not need moist air. Other varieties of Polystichum are more difficult to grow
Common name: Tsusina Holly Fern

PTERIS
Pteris produces handsome fronds (leaves) in a range of shapes and sizes. The most popular types are varieties of **P. cretica** — the Table Fern. Slender leaflets are borne on thread-like stalks. **Albolineata** is variegated, **wilsonii** is feathery-tipped and **alexandrae** is cockscomb-tipped. The prettiest Table Fern is **P. ensiformis victoriae** (silver banded along the midrib). **P. tremula** is quite different — the fronds are large and feathery
Common name: Pteris

RADERMACHERA DANIELLE
A house plant introduced to Europe at the beginning of the 1980s. The large leaves of these tree-like plants are divided into shiny pointed leaflets. Radermachera tolerates central heating
Common name: Radermachera

RHAPIS EXCELSA
The most popular Fan Palm — it is small enough for an average-sized room. The fronds (leaves) are divided into segments to give a fan-like effect. A white-striped variety is available
Common name: Little Lady Palm

RHOEO DISCOLOR
The short stem bears fleshy, lance-shaped leaves. Their colouring is unusual — glossy green or green-and-yellow above, purple below. Small white flowers in purple 'boats' appear at the base of the lower leaves
Common name: Boat Lily

PILEA CADIEREI
Aluminium Plant

PIPER CROCATUM
Ornamental Pepper

PLATYCERIUM BIFURCATUM
Staghorn Fern

PLECTRANTHUS OERTENDAHLII
Swedish Ivy

PODOCARPUS MACROPHYLLUS
Buddhist Pine

PLANT DETAILS		HOUSE PLANT RECORD					Easy or difficult
Dimensions	Family group	Variety grown	Year of arrival	Supplier	Performance during the year		
Depends on the species	Evergreen Foliage Plant						Easy
Height 5 ft Leaves 3–5 in. long	Evergreen Foliage Plant						Moderately difficult
Leaves 3 ft long	Evergreen Foliage Plant — Fern						Moderately easy
Leaves 1–2 in. long	Evergreen Foliage Plant						Moderately easy
Leaves 6 in. long	Evergreen Foliage Plant Dracaena Group						Moderately difficult
Height 6 ft — Leaves 3 in. long	Evergreen Foliage Plant						Easy
Leaves 1–2 ft long	Evergreen Foliage Plant — Fern						Moderately easy
Depends on the species	Evergreen Foliage Plant						Difficult
Leaves 1 ft long	Evergreen Foliage Plant — Fern						Moderately easy
Depends on the species	Evergreen Foliage Plant — Fern						Moderately easy
Leaflets 1 in. long	Evergreen Foliage Plant						Moderately easy
Height 4 ft — Leaflets 8 in. long	Evergreen Foliage Plant — Palm						Moderately easy
Leaves 1 ft long	Evergreen Foliage Plant						Moderately difficult

VARIETIES

POLYPODIUM AUREUM
Hare's Foot Fern

POLYSCIAS BALFOURIANA
Dinner Plate Aralia

PTERIS CRETICA
Table Fern

RHAPIS EXCELSA
Little Lady Palm

RHOEO DISCOLOR
Boat Lily

FOLIAGE PLANTS

Varieties

Variety	Common name	Light	Air humidity	Warmth	Water: Growing period	Water: Resting period
RHOICISSUS Grape Ivy (**R. rhomboidea**) is one of the most popular of all climbing house plants. Each leaf is made up of three 2 in. long leaflets. For something a little different choose the variety **Ellen Danica** (lobed leaflets) or **Jubilee** (large, dark green leaflets). **R. capensis** (Cape Grape) is quite different — each 8 in. long leaf is undivided, glossy and brown-edged	Rhoicissus	semi-shade	moist	warm	●●●	●
SANSEVIERIA This tough plant deserves its universal popularity. It will grow in bright sunshine or shade, withstand dry air, draughts and periods without water and rarely needs repotting. The favourite variety is the golden-edged **S. trifasciata laurentii**. Not all species of Sansevieria are tall and upright — **S. hahnii** and its varieties are compact rosettes composed of 4 in. long leaves	Mother-in-Law's Tongue	sun/semi-shade	dry	warm	●●	●
SAXIFRAGA SARMENTOSA The outstanding feature is the production of long red runners which bear miniature plantlets at their ends. Leaves are silvery-veined — more attractive but more difficult is the green-, white- and pink-leaved variety **tricolor**	Mother of Thousands	semi-shade	moist	warm	●●●	●
SCHEFFLERA ACTINOPHYLLA A tree-like plant bearing leaves in which glossy leaflets radiate from the top of the leaf stalks like umbrella spokes. An attractive bush when young, but becoming lanky with age	Umbrella Tree	semi-shade	moist	warm	●●●	●
SCINDAPSUS AUREUS Devil's Ivy (U.S. name Pothos) is similar to but more colourful than Philodendron scandens. The heart-shaped leaves of this climber are flecked with yellow. More colourful, but much more difficult are **Golden Queen** (nearly all-yellow) and **Marble Queen** (nearly all-white)	Devil's Ivy	semi-shade	moist	warm	●●●	●
SEDUM Sedums are generally low growing with branching stems and an abundance of fleshy leaves. **S. pachyphyllum** (Jelly Beans) is a typical and popular example — 1 ft tall stems with 1 in. long red-tipped leaves. There are two popular trailers. **S. morganianum** (Donkey's Tail) bears 2–3 ft long trailing stems clothed with cylindrical leaves. **S. sieboldii mediovariegatum** has thin stems with variegated leaves in clusters of three	Sedum	sun	dry	warm	●●●	●
SELAGINELLA A Victorian favourite which has lost its popularity. Useful in a terrarium but it is too delicate for the sideboard — the tiny leaves shrivel in dry air or draughts. There are **S. uncinata** (blue-green) and **S. martensii** (pale green)	Creeping Moss	semi-shade	moist	hot	●●	●
SEMPERVIVUM Sempervivum is an old favourite. It is completely hardy — this plant seems to thrive on neglect so do not overwater, overfeed or repot unnecessarily. The popular type is **S. arachnoideum** with its dense covering of threads	Houseleek	sun	dry	warm	●●	●
SENECIO MACROGLOSSUS It is surprising that the Senecio Ivies are not more widely grown. They are less affected than Hedera varieties by dry air, and small daisy-like flowers appear. The popular type is the yellow-blotched variety **variegatus**	Cape Ivy	sun/semi-shade	moist	warm	●●	●
SENECIO ROWLEYANUS The leaves are green and spherical, strung together on long thread-like stems. The leaves on this species are distinctly pea-like — on **S. citriformis** they are lemon-shaped and oval on **S. herreianus**	String of Beads	sun	dry	warm	●●	●
SETCREASEA PURPUREA A straggly plant which makes up for its untidiness by its attractive colour — a rich purple when grown in good light. The leaves are slightly hairy and in spring deep pink flowers appear in clusters	Purple Heart	sun/semi-shade	moist	warm	●●●	●
SONERILA MARGARITACEA A bushy, colourful plant — red stems bear leaves which are patterned with silver above and coloured purple below. This is one for the terrarium — it is too delicate for ordinary room conditions	Frosted Sonerila	semi-shade	moist	hot	●●	●

RHOICISSUS RHOMBOIDEA
Grape Ivy

SANSEVIERIA TRIFASCIATA LAURENTII
Mother-in-Law's Tongue

SAXIFRAGA SARMENTOSA TRICOLOR
Mother of Thousands

SCHEFFLERA ACTINOPHYLLA
Umbrella Tree

SCINDAPSUS AUREUS
Devil's Ivy

Plant Details		House Plant Record				Easy or difficult
Dimensions	Family group	Variety grown	Year of arrival	Supplier	Performance during the year	
Depends on the species	Evergreen Foliage Plant — Vine					Easy
Leaves 3 ft long	Evergreen Foliage Plant — Succulent					Easy
Height 2–3 ft — Leaves 1½ in. long	Evergreen Foliage Plant					Easy
Height 6 ft — Leaflets 6 in. long	Evergreen Foliage Plant					Moderately easy
Height 6 ft — Leaves 4–6 in. long	Evergreen Foliage Plant					Moderately easy
Depends on the species	Evergreen Foliage Plant — Succulent					Moderately easy
Depends on the species	Evergreen Foliage Plant					Difficult
Height 1 in.	Evergreen Foliage Plant — Succulent					Easy
Height 10 ft — Leaves 3 in. long	Evergreen Foliage Plant — Succulent					Moderately easy
Height 3 ft — Leaves ¼ in. long	Evergreen Foliage Plant — Succulent					Easy
Height 1½ ft — Leaves 5 in. long	Evergreen Foliage Plant — Tradescantia Group					Easy
Leaves 3 in. long	Evergreen Foliage Plant					Difficult

SEDUM PACHYPHYLLUM
Jelly Beans

SEMPERVIVUM ARACHNOIDEUM
Cobweb Houseleek

SENECIO MACROGLOSSUS VARIEGATUS
Cape Ivy

SENECIO ROWLEYANUS
String of Beads

SONERILA MARGARITACEA
Frosted Sonerila

FOLIAGE PLANTS

Varieties

Common name	CONDITIONS REQUIRED			Water:	
	Light	Air humidity	Warmth	Growing period	Resting period

STROBILANTHES DYERANUS
A lovely shrub when young — the long, pointed leaves are dark green with a silvery-purple sheen. Unfortunately this fades with age — discard old plants and replace with new stock raised from cuttings
— *Persian Shield*

SYNGONIUM PODOPHYLLUM
An unusual feature is the marked change in leaf shape as the plant gets older. The young arrow-shaped leaves are borne on stiff stalks. With age it becomes a climber with lobed leaves. Many variegated varieties are available
— *Goosefoot Plant*

TETRASTIGMA VOINIERIANUM
The Chestnut Vine is the giant of the house plant vines. The five leaflets which make up each 1 ft leaf are glossy and saw-edged. A rampant grower (5 ft per year) used for covering large areas
— *Chestnut Vine*

TILLANDSIA
During the 1980s there was an upsurge in interest in the Air Plants or Grey Tillandsias. These plants bear furry scales on their leaves — these scales absorb water from the air and nutrients from dust. The commonest is **T. usneoides** (Spanish Moss). Others include **T. ionantha** and **T. caput-medusae**. Short-lived flowers appear. Mist occasionally but do not water
— *Air Plant*

TOLMIEA MENZIESII
A compact mound of downy, bright green leaves — it is one of the hardiest of all house plants. Plantlets form at the base of the long-stalked leaves. This plant does badly in hot, dry air
— *Piggyback Plant*

TRADESCANTIA
The most popular of all hanging plants — the bases of the striped oval leaves clasp the stem. The most popular species is **T. fluminensis** — the variety **variegata** is cream-striped, **Quicksilver** is white-striped. **T. albiflora** is similar but the underside is not purple. There are a number of varieties bearing white, mauve or yellow stripes. The large-leaved Tradescantia is **T. blossfeldiana**
— *Wandering Jew*

WASHINGTONIA FILIFERA
A large Fan Palm — easily recognised by the fibrous threads at the edges of the leaflets. This one is not suitable for an average-sized room — it is too wide-spreading. Short-lived, so get Chamaerops if you want a large Fan Palm
— *Desert Fan Palm*

YUCCA ELEPHANTIPES
A fine false palm which bears a crown of sword-like leaves on top of a stout trunk. It needs space and cool winter conditions — white bell-shaped flowers may appear after a number of years
— *Spineless Yucca*

ZEBRINA PENDULA
Zebrina is similar to Tradescantia but more colourful. The leaves are glistening and multicoloured above and purple below. The surface may be green and silver (**Z. pendula**), green and purple (**Z. pendula purpusii**) or green, silver, pink and red (**Z. pendula quadricolor**)
— *Zebrina*

STROBILANTHES DYERANUS
Persian Shield

SYNGONIUM PODOPHYLLUM
Goosefoot Plant

TOLMIEA MENZIESII
Piggyback Plant

TRADESCANTIA FLUMINENSIS VARIEGATA
Wandering Jew

ZEBRINA PENDULA
Silvery Inch Plant

PLANT DETAILS		HOUSE PLANT RECORD				Easy or difficult
mensions	Family group	Variety grown	Year of arrival	Supplier	Performance during the year	
Leaves 5 in. long	Temporary Foliage Plant					Difficult
Height 6 ft	Evergreen Foliage Plant					Moderately easy
Leaflets 6 in. long	Evergreen Foliage Plant — Vine					Easy
Depends on the species	Evergreen Foliage Plant — Bromeliad					Easy
Height 9 in. — Leaves 2 in. long	Evergreen Foliage Plant					Easy
Height 1–2 ft — Leaves –3 in. long	Evergreen Foliage Plant — Tradescantia Group					Easy
Leaves 3 ft long	Evergreen Foliage Plant — Palm					Moderately easy
Height 5 ft — Leaves 3 ft long	Evergreen Foliage Plant					Moderately easy
Height 2 ft — Leaves –3 in. long	Evergreen Foliage Plant — Tradescantia Group					Easy

VARIETIES

FLOWERING PLANTS

Varieties

	CONDITIONS REQUIRED					
Common name	Light	Air humidity	Warmth	Water: Growing period		Resting period

ABUTILON
Pendent bells on slender stalks. **A. megapotamicum** is a 4 ft climber/trailer which bears lantern-like blooms in summer. **A. hybridum** is a spreading 5 ft tree with bell-like flowers in spring and summer — white, yellow, pink and red are available
Abutilon

ACACIA ARMATA
A useful shrub where space is not a problem, but it has never been popular. **A. armata** bears 1 in. long spiny leaves (really modified leaf stalks). In spring the yellow ball-like flower-heads appear. **A. dealbata** is the florists 'Mimosa'
Kangaroo Thorn

ACALYPHA HISPIDA
Brightly-coloured flower spikes hang like tassels from the stems. These pendent spikes appear amongst the 6 in. long leaves, each spike bearing hundreds of tiny red flowers. **Alba** is an unusual white variety
Chenille Plant

ACHIMENES HYBRIDA
Short-lived, trumpet-like flared flowers appear from early summer to mid autumn. Much used in hanging baskets — red, pink, purple, blue, white and yellow varieties are available. Store rhizomes after flowering has finished
Cupid's Bower

AECHMEA FASCIATA
The Aechmeas are typical Bromeliads with leathery, arching leaves and a distinct central 'vase'. **A. fasciata** is by far the most popular — the pink ball-like flower-head is borne above the 2 ft long grey-green leaves. There are other species — **A. chantinii** has orange flowers and **A. fulgens discolor** has red berries
Urn Plant

AESCHYNANTHUS LOBBIANUS
Oval-leaved trailing plants which are difficult to grow. The best known is **A. lobbianus** — tubular red flowers push out of brown 'lipstick cases'. **A. speciosus** is larger — 3 in. long red and yellow flowers stand erect
Lipstick Vine

AGAPANTHUS AFRICANUS
You will need space for this one. The ball-like heads of blue flowers are borne on 2 ft stalks during the summer. In winter keep the plant cool — very little water is needed
Blue African Lily

ANANAS COMOSUS
The Common Pineapple (**A. comosus**) and its yellow-striped form **variegatus** will produce pink flowers on mature plants. These are followed by small pink fruits (aromatic but not edible) if conditions are warm and humid
Pineapple

ANTHURIUM
The flowers are exotic — large 'palettes' with coloured tails at the centre. Choose the red **A. scherzerianum** (Flamingo Flower) — spear-shaped leaves, coiled tails. The taller, straight-tailed **A. andreanum** is even more difficult to grow
Anthurium

APHELANDRA SQUARROSA
The flower-head is made up of yellow bracts — the 9 in. long glossy leaves are prominently veined in white or ivory. The usual variety is **louisae**. Difficult to grow for more than a few months
Zebra Plant

ARDISIA CRENATA
The glossy leaves make this slow-growing shrub an attractive foliage plant, but its main feature is the presence of red berries at Christmas. These follow the tiny white flowers which appear in summer
Coral Berry

ACACIA ARMATA
Kangaroo Thorn

ACALYPHA HISPIDA
Chenille Plant

ACHIMENES HYBRIDA
Cupid's Bower

AECHMEA CHANTINII
Amazonian Zebra Plant

AECHMEA FASCIATA
Urn Plant

Flowering plants are grown in the home primarily for the display provided by their blooms and/or fruits. There are two basic groups. The Flowering House Plants are varieties which are capable of living permanently under room conditions, provided that their cultural needs are met. Not all remain a year-round attraction. After flowering the foliage may provide little interest and some varieties need to overwinter in an unheated room. The second group are the Temporary Pot Plants, which have a limited display period and are removed after flowering. Most are discarded at this stage, but some can be stored indoors as leafless plants or bulbs and others can be transferred outdoors into the garden. The indoor flowering period of this group is prolonged by good care, but flower and leaf loss are inevitable and it is not your fault.

PLANT DETAILS		HOUSE PLANT RECORD					Easy or difficult
Dimensions	Family group	Variety grown	Year of arrival	Supplier	Performance during the year		
Flowers 2 in. long	Flowering House Plant						Moderately easy
Height 4–6 ft Flower-heads ½ in. across	Flowering House Plant						Difficult
Height 5 ft — Flower spikes 1½ ft long	Flowering House Plant						Difficult
Height 9 in.	Temporary Pot Plant						Moderately easy
Flower-heads 6 in. across	Flowering House Plant — Bromeliad						Moderately easy
Height 2 ft — Flowers 2 in. long	Flowering House Plant						Difficult
Flower-heads 4–8 in. across	Flowering House Plant						Moderately easy
Flower stalks 2–3 ft high	Flowering House Plant						Moderately difficult
Flowers 2–4 in. long	Flowering House Plant						Difficult
Flower-heads 4–6 in. long	Flowering House Plant						Difficult
Height 3 ft	Flowering House Plant						Moderately easy

VARIETIES

AESCHYNANTHUS LOBBIANUS
Lipstick Vine

ANANAS COMOSUS VARIEGATUS
Ivory Pineapple

ANTHURIUM SCHERZERIANUM
Flamingo Flower

APHELANDRA SQUARROSA LOUISAE
Zebra Plant

ARDISIA CRENATA
Coral Berry

FLOWERING PLANTS

Varieties

	Common name	Light	Air humidity	Warmth	Water: Growing period	Water: Resting period
AZALEA INDICA — A popular Christmas plant — proper name **Rhododendron simsii**. Blooms may be single or double in white, pink, red or orange. Choose a plant with lots of buds and a few open flowers. Keep the plants well lit, cool and wet at all times. Stand the pot in the garden from late spring to autumn	Azalea	semi-shade	low	cool	●●●	●●
BEGONIA — The flowering evergreen Begonias are less spectacular than the Temporary Pot Plant types (see below) but they keep their leaves all year round. The most popular bushy type is the Wax Begonia (**B. semperflorens**) — a rounded bush 6–12 in. high with 1 in. flowers. Less common are the trailing ones (e.g **B. glaucophylla**) and the tall cane-stemmed types such as **B. lucerna**	Begonia	semi-shade	low	warm	●●	●
BEGONIA — Some Begonias are bought as temporary residents to provide a splash of winter colour or summer display. The most spectacular are the Tuberous Begonias, including the large-flowering **B. tuberhybrida** and the smaller-flowering **B. multiflora**. Another group includes the Lorraine Begonias — Christmas favourites for generations. A third group has become popular in recent years — the Hiemalis Hybrids have 2 in. bright flowers (e.g **B. Fireglow**). They can be bought in bloom at any time of the year	Begonia	semi-shade	low	warm	●●●	—
BELOPERONE GUTTATA — Salmon-coloured, prawn-shaped flower-heads appear at the end of arching stems — these may appear at any time of the year. Cut back stems to half size each spring to maintain bushiness	Shrimp Plant	sun	high	cool	●●●	●
BILLBERGIA NUTANS — The easiest Bromeliad to grow — young plants flower quite readily. The grass-like leaves are about 1 ft long. In early spring the arching flower-heads appear, with tiny flowers below the showy pink bracts	Queen's Tears	some sun	high	cool	●●	●●
BOUGAINVILLEA GLABRA — A showy climbing plant with brightly-coloured, papery bracts. The basic species is **B. glabra**, but its hybrids are more popular. Top of the list is the large-leaved, large-flowered **B. buttiana Mrs Butt** (red)	Paper Flower	sun	high	cool	●●	●
BROWALLIA — The Bush Violet is usually bought in flower, but it can be easily raised from seed. With care the flowering period lasts for many weeks. **B. speciosa** bears violet tubular flowers with white throats	Bush Violet	some sun	high	cool	●●	—
BRUNFELSIA CALYCINA — The white-eyed fragrant flowers change colour — yesterday's purple, today's pale violet and tomorrow's white. The plant grows about 2 ft tall — its main hate is a sudden change in temperature. Keep compact by pruning	Yesterday, Today and Tomorrow	semi-shade	high	cool	●●	●
CALCEOLARIA HERBEOHYBRIDA — The soft leaves are large and hairy and the springtime flowers are curious and colourful. They are pouched-shaped in yellow, orange, red or white with dark-coloured spots. Flowering period lasts about a month	Slipper Flower	semi-shade	low	cool	●●●	—
CALLISTEMON CITRINUS — **C. citrinus** will reach about 3 ft high and in summer the cylindrical flower spikes appear on top of the stems. No petals, just yellow-tipped red stamens. The leaves are bronzy when young	Bottlebrush Plant	sun	low	cool	●●●	
CAMELLIA JAPONICA — A beauty — but extremely temperamental. It needs cool conditions without any sudden changes in temperature or soil moisture. The large blooms are single or double in a wide variety of colours	Camellia	some sun	low	cool	●●	●●
CAMPANULA ISOPHYLLA — One of the best of all summer-flowering trailing plants — 1 ft long stems bear a profusion of star-shaped flowers. Cut back after flowering. The species has blue flowers — the variety **alba** is white	Italian Bellflower	some sun	high	cool	●●●	●

AZALEA INDICA
Azalea

BEGONIA MULTIFLORA
Tuberous Begonia

BEGONIA SEMPERFLORENS
Wax Begonia

BELOPERONE GUTTATA
Shrimp Plant

BILLBERGIA NUTANS
Queen's Tears

PLANT DETAILS		HOUSE PLANT RECORD					Easy or difficult
Dimensions	Family group	Variety grown	Year of arrival	Supplier	Performance during the year		
Height 1–1½ ft — Flowers 1½–2 in. across	Temporary Pot Plant						Moderately difficult
Depends on the species	Flowering House Plant						Depends on the species
Depends on the species	Temporary Pot Plant						Moderately difficult
Flower-heads 4 in. long	Flowering House Plant						Easy
Flower stalks 1–2 ft high	Flowering House Plant — Bromeliad						Easy
Flowers 1 in. across	Flowering House Plant						Difficult
Flowers 2 in. across	Temporary Pot Plant						Moderately easy
Height 2 ft — Flowers 2 in. across	Flowering House Plant						Moderately difficult
Flowers 1–2 in. across	Temporary Pot Plant						Moderately easy
Height 3 ft — Flower-heads 3 in. long	Flowering House Plant						Easy
Flowers 3–5 in. across	Flowering House Plant						Difficult
Flowers 1½ in. across	Flowering House Plant						Moderately easy

VARIETIES

BOUGAINVILLEA GLABRA
Paper Flower

BROWALLIA SPECIOSA
Bush Violet

BRUNFELSIA CALYCINA
Yesterday, Today and Tomorrow

CAMELLIA JAPONICA
Camellia

CAMPANULA ISOPHYLLA
Italian Bellflower

Varieties

FLOWERING PLANTS

	Common name	CONDITIONS REQUIRED				
		Light	Air humidity	Warmth	Water: Growing period	Water: Resting period

CAPSICUM ANNUUM
The usual time to buy Capsicum is in December for the festive season — the colourful cone-shaped fruits should remain for two or three months. They change from green to yellow and finally red

Common name: Christmas Pepper

CELOSIA
There are two distinct types of this showy pot plant. **C. plumosa** (Plume Flower) bears red or yellow plumes in summer — dwarfs (8–12 in.) are available. **C. cristata** has yellow, orange or red cockscomb-like flower-heads

Common name: Celosia

CESTRUM
Tall, weak-stemmed plants which are more suited to the conservatory than to the living room. The flowers are tubular and the fragrance is intense. Cestrums are rare — you will have to search for **C. elegans** (red), **C. auranticum** (orange) or **C. nocturnum** (white)

Common name: Jessamine

CHRYSANTHEMUM
The Pot Chrysanthemum has become a favourite pot plant. It can be bought in bloom at any time of the year in any colour but blue. Pick plants with a mass of buds showing colour — they should stay in bloom for 6–8 weeks. **C. frutescens** (Marguerite) is summer flowering — Charm and Cascade Chrysanthemums have flowers which are much smaller but far more numerous than other varieties

Common name: Pot Chrysanthemum

CINERARIA
Cineraria (proper name **Senecio cruentus**) is a popular gift plant — masses of daisy-like flowers cover the soft leaves which are up to 8 in. across. The colour range is impressive — white, blue, pink, purple and red. Buy plants with lots of buds and a few open blooms. Kept in a cool room they should last 4–6 weeks

Common name: Cineraria

CITRUS
There are a few dwarf varieties which can be relied upon to form oranges or lemons indoors. **C. mitis** (Calamondin Orange) is the most popular — white, fragrant flowers followed by 1½ in. diameter bitter oranges appear at any time of the year. Other types include Sweet Orange (**C. sinensis**) and Lemon (**C. limon meyeri**)

Common name: Orange or Lemon

CLERODENDRUM THOMSONIAE
A weak-stemmed climber — prune in winter to produce a compact bush or hanging basket plant. The inflated flowers (white with a red tip) appear in summer amongst the heart-shaped leaves

Common name: Glory Bower

CLIANTHUS FORMOSUS
Large, claw-like red flowers are borne in clusters in late spring or summer. This low-growing shrub is short-lived, usually dying after flowering. The climbing Clianthus (**C. puniceus**) is a conservatory plant

Common name: Glory Pea

CLIVIA MINIATA
Clusters of 10–20 flowers appear in early spring on top of a tall stalk. Orange is the usual colour but red, yellow and cream are available. For annual flowering keep cool, unfed and quite dry in winter

Common name: Kaffir Lily

COLUMNEA
A colourful hanging basket plant which blooms in winter or early spring. The 3 ft long stems bear tubular flowers — usually red with yellow markings. A difficult plant — if you are a beginner, choose an easier one such as **C. Stavanger** or **C. banksii** rather than the more popular **C. gloriosa**

Common name: Goldfish Plant

CONVALLARIA MAJALIS
Dainty white bells appear at Christmas or in early spring. Buy crowns which have been prepared for indoor use. Plant in compost — these will come into flower 4–6 weeks after planting. **Fortin's Giant** is a recommended strain. Discard after flowering

Common name: Lily of the Valley

CRINUM POWELLII
Everything about Crinum is extraordinarily large — the 6 in. bulb, the 3 ft flower stalk and leaves and the 7 in. long trumpets in white, pink or red which appear in late summer. The display lasts 4–5 weeks

Common name: Swamp Lily

CAPSICUM ANNUUM
Christmas Pepper

CELOSIA PLUMOSA
Plume Flower

CHRYSANTHEMUM MORIFOLIUM
Pot Chrysanthemum

CINERARIA (SENECIO CRUENTUS)
Cineraria

CITRUS MITIS
Calamondin Orange

VARIETIES

PLANT DETAILS		HOUSE PLANT RECORD					Easy or difficult
Dimensions	Family group	Variety grown	Year of arrival	Supplier	Performance during the year		
Fruits 1–2 in. long	Temporary Pot Plant						Moderately easy
Height 1½–2 ft	Temporary Pot Plant						Moderately easy
Height 10 ft	Flowering House Plant						Moderately difficult
Height 1–2 ft	Temporary Pot Plant						Moderately easy
Flowers 1–3 in. across	Temporary Pot Plant						Moderately easy
Height 3–4 ft	Flowering House Plant						Moderately difficult
Height 8 ft — Flowers 1 in. long	Flowering House Plant						Difficult
Height 2 ft — Flowers 2 in. long	Temporary Pot Plant						Difficult
Leaves 1½ ft long Flowers 3 in. across	Flowering House Plant						Moderately easy
Flowers 2½–3 in. across	Flowering House Plant						Difficult
Leaves 8 in. long Flowers ¼ in. long	Temporary Pot Plant						Moderately easy
Flowers 6 in. across	Flowering House Plant						Moderately easy

CLERODENDRUM THOMSONIAE
Glory Bower

CLIANTHUS FORMOSUS
Glory Pea

CLIVIA MINIATA
Kaffir Lily

COLUMNEA GLORIOSA
Goldfish Plant

CONVALLARIA MAJALIS
Lily of the Valley

FLOWERING PLANTS

Varieties

Varieties	Common name	Light	Air humidity	Warmth	Water: Growing period	Water: Resting period
CROCUS Crocus corms are planted in the autumn for flowering in early spring. The varieties of **C. chrysanthus** are often yellow, but pale blues and mauves also occur, often with a golden base. The deep blues and whites are varieties of **C. vernus** — the flowers are larger and they bloom a few weeks later	Crocus	bright	mist	cool	2 drops	—
CROSSANDRA UNDULIFOLIA The tubular orange flowers appear from spring until autumn on top of 1–2 ft high flower stalks. Moist air around the leaves is a must — so is dead-heading to prolong the flowering season	Firecracker Plant	semi-shade	humid	cool	2 drops	1 drop
CUPHEA IGNEA A 1 ft bush which produces flowers from spring to late autumn. These blooms are interesting rather than spectacular — thin red tubes with white and purple tips. Cut back in early spring	Cigar Plant	semi-shade	dry	cool	2 drops	1 drop
CYCLAMEN PERSICUM Swept-back flowers on long stalks above decorative foliage which is usually edged, marbled or lined in white. The blooms may be plain, frilled or perfumed. Most plants are consigned to the dustbin after a couple of weeks, but with care the display can last for several months. Buy in autumn, not midwinter — make sure there are plenty of unopened buds. Stand on a north-facing windowsill in a cool room	Cyclamen	bright	humid	cool	2 drops	—
CYTISUS Cytisus outdoors is called Broom — indoors it is Genista. Long sprays of fragrant yellow flowers appear in spring at the end of arching stems. Choose **C. racemosus** rather than **C. canariensis**. The pot must be placed outdoors during summer	Genista	semi-shade	mist	cool	3 drops	—
DAHLIA Pot Dahlias are much less popular than Pot Chrysanthemums, but they are beginning to appear at garden centres. They are hybrids of **D. variabilis** and grow about 1 ft high. Pot Dahlias can be raised from seed — they are listed as Bedding Dahlias in the catalogues	Pot Dahlia	semi-shade	humid	cool	3 drops	—
DIANTHUS You may occasionally find Dianthus for sale as a house plant but you will not find it in the textbooks. The Annual Pinks are hybrids of **D. chinensis** — look for **Baby Doll**, **Snowflake** and **Telstar**. The Annual Carnations (hybrids of **D. caryophyllus**) have blooms which are larger and double	Dianthus	semi-shade	mist	cool	2 drops	—
DIPLADENIA Large petunia-like flowers appear in summer on the twining stems. A natural climber — cut back after flowering to grow as a bush. **D. sanderi rosea** produces yellow-throated, pink trumpets — **D. (Mandevilla) splendens** has pink-throated flowers	Dipladenia	bright	humid	warm	2 drops	1 drop
DUCHESNEA INDICA Vigorous, quite hardy but hard to find. Trailing runners and bright yellow flowers are present in summer. The strawberry-like fruits appear later — edible, but tasteless. Keep cool but frost-free in winter	Indian Strawberry	bright	mist	cool	3 drops	—
EPISCIA There are two types — both are attractive trailing plants which bloom throughout the summer. **E. cupreata** (Flame Violet) has small red flowers amongst silvery-veined leaves — **E. dianthiflora** (Lace Flower) has frilly-edged white flowers and velvety foliage	Episcia	semi-shade	humid	cool	2 drops	—
ERICA Heathers are shrubby plants bought in flower in winter. Do not buy one unless you can provide a cool and well-lit spot. Never let the compost dry out. Choose **E. gracilis** (ball-like flowers) or **E. hyemalis** (tubular flowers)	Heather	semi-shade	humid	cool	3 drops	—
EUCHARIS GRANDIFLORA The flowers appear in late summer and again a few months later if conditions are favourable. Each fragrant white bloom looks like a narcissus with a spiky trumpet. Three or more are borne on a 2 ft stalk	Amazon Lily	bright	mist	warm	3 drops	2 drops

CROCUS VERNUS
Crocus

CROSSANDRA UNDULIFOLIA
Firecracker Plant

CUPHEA IGNEA
Cigar Plant

CYCLAMEN PERSICUM
Cyclamen

CYTISUS RACEMOSUS
Genista

PLANT DETAILS		HOUSE PLANT RECORD					Easy or difficult
Dimensions	Family group	Variety grown	Year of arrival	Supplier	Performance during the year		
Flowers 3–5 in. long	Temporary Pot Plant						Moderately easy
Height 1–2 ft — Flowers 1½ in. across	Flowering House Plant						Moderately difficult
Height 1 ft — Flowers 1 in. long	Flowering House Plant						Moderately easy
Flowers 1–2 in. long	Temporary Pot Plant						Moderately easy
Flowers ¾ in. long	Temporary Pot Plant						Moderately easy
Height 1 ft — Flowers 2 in. across	Temporary Pot Plant						Moderately easy
Flowers 1½–2 in. across	Temporary Pot Plant						Moderately easy
Flowers 3 in. across	Flowering House Plant						Moderately difficult
Fruits ¾ in. across	Flowering House Plant						Easy
Flowers ¾–1½ in. across	Flowering House Plant						Difficult
Height 1½–2 ft — Flowers 3–¼ in. across	Temporary Pot Plant						Moderately difficult
Height 2 ft — Flowers 3 in. across	Flowering House Plant						Moderately difficult

VARIETIES

DAHLIA VARIABILIS
Pot Dahlia

DIANTHUS CHINENSIS
Annual Pink

DIPLADENIA SANDERI ROSEA
Dipladenia

DUCHESNEA INDICA
Indian Strawberry

EPISCIA DIANTHIFLORA
Lace Flower

ERICA GRACILIS
Cape Heath

FLOWERING PLANTS

Varieties

Varieties	Common name	Light	Air humidity	Warmth	Water: Growing period	Water: Resting period
EUPHORBIA MILII — An excellent and undemanding choice for a sunny window. The grooved stems bear short spines — leaves may drop in winter but new leaf buds soon appear. The flower-heads are borne from early spring to midsummer — red is the popular colour but salmon and yellow types are available. The sap is poisonous	Crown of Thorns	☀	○	🌡	💧💧	💧
EXACUM AFFINE — Buy this one as a pot plant or raise from seed. A small and bushy plant with flowers which are pale purple with a gold centre. These blooms are abundant and fragrant — the flowering season lasts for months	Arabian Violet				💧💧💧	—
FUCHSIA — There are hundreds of named varieties of **F. hybrida**, with the familiar hooped-skirt flowers hanging from the stems. These blooms may be single, semi-double or double, with colour combinations of white, pink, red and purple. A collection can provide flowers from spring to autumn. Most plants are thrown away after the flowers and leaves fall, but they can be overwintered in a cool room	Fuchsia				💧💧💧	
GARDENIA JASMINOIDES — The blooms are semi-double or double and the white or cream petals are waxy. The fragrance is very strong and the glossy leaves make Gardenia an attractive plant when not in flower. Unfortunately it is extremely temperamental	Gardenia				💧💧	
GERBERA JAMESONII — The daisy-like flowers are in many striking colours and both single and double forms are available. The flower stalks are 2 ft high — a compact strain such as **Happipot** or **Parade** should be chosen	Barbeton Daisy				💧💧💧	—
GLORIOSA ROTHSCHILDIANA — A spectacular climber which bears tendrils at the tips of the leaves. In summer the lily-like flowers appear — red, swept-back petals with a yellow base. Buy it in flower or raise from a tuber	Glory Lily				💧💧💧	—
GLOXINIA — The bell-shaped velvety blooms have plain or ruffled petals in a variety of colours — white, pink, red or purple. Choose a plant with plenty of unopened buds — the display should last for 2 months or more	Gloxinia				💧💧	—
GUZMANIA — The best known Guzmania is **G. lingulata minor**. The smooth-edged arching leaves are 4 in. long and there are various flower forms — red or orange like **Amaranth** and **Grand Prix** or yellow-tipped like **Marlebeca**	Scarlet Star				💧💧	💧💧
HAEMANTHUS KATHARINAE — Blood Lily is a spectacular plant — a stout stalk appears in summer, carrying the large globe of red tubular flowers above the large leaves at the base. Some Blood Lilies lose their leaves in winter — this one is evergreen	Blood Lily				💧💧	💧
HELIOTROPIUM HYBRIDUM — An excellent but little-used shrub for indoor decoration — the large heads of tiny purple, blue or white flowers will perfume a room throughout the summer months. It is best to raise new cuttings each year, as the plant soon deteriorates	Heliotrope				💧💧💧	💧
HIBISCUS ROSA-SINENSIS — Numerous named varieties in white, yellow, orange, pink and red are available. Hibiscus is becoming popular as a specimen plant for a sunny windowsill. Each large papery flower with a prominent central column lasts for only a day or two, but with proper care there will be a succession from spring to autumn	Rose of China				💧💧	💧
HIPPEASTRUM HYBRIDA — Clusters of trumpet-shaped flowers appear on top of a stout stalk in spring. The strap-like leaves emerge after the flowers appear. This plant is usually bought as a large bulb in autumn. Usually discarded when the blooms have faded, but it can be kept for next year	Amaryllis				💧💧💧	💧

CONDITIONS REQUIRED

EUPHORBIA MILII — Crown of Thorns

EXACUM AFFINE — Arabian Violet

FUCHSIA HYBRIDA — Fuchsia

GARDENIA JASMINOIDES — Gardenia

GERBERA JAMESONII — Barbeton Daisy

PLANT DETAILS		HOUSE PLANT RECORD					Easy or difficult
Dimensions	Family group	Variety grown	Year of arrival	Supplier	Performance during the year		
Height 3 ft — Flowers ½ in. across	Flowering House Plant						Easy
Flowers ½ in. across	Temporary Pot Plant						Moderately easy
Flowers 1½–3 in. long	Temporary Pot Plant						Moderately easy
Height 1½ ft — Flowers 3 in. across	Temporary Pot Plant						Difficult
Flowers 2 in. across	Temporary Pot Plant						Moderately easy
Height 4 ft — Flowers 4 in. long	Temporary Pot Plant						Moderately difficult
Flowers 3 in. across	Temporary Pot Plant						Moderately difficult
Flower-heads 3 in. across	Flowering House Plant — Bromeliad						Moderately easy
Flower-heads 8 in. across	Flowering House Plant						Moderately easy
Flower-heads 4–6 in. across	Temporary Pot Plant						Easy
Flowers 4–5 in. across	Flowering House Plant						Moderately difficult
Flowers 5–6 in. across	Temporary Pot Plant						Easy

VARIETIES

GLOXINIA
(SINNINGIA SPECIOSA)
Gloxinia

GUZMANIA LINGULATA MINOR
Scarlet Star

HELIOTROPIUM HYBRIDUM
Heliotrope

HIBISCUS ROSA-SINENSIS
Rose of China

HIPPEASTRUM HYBRIDA
Amaryllis

FLOWERING PLANTS

Varieties

	Common name	CONDITIONS REQUIRED				
		Light	Air humidity	Warmth	Water: Growing period	Water: Resting period
HOYA CARNOSA A vigorous climber — the twining stems can reach 15 ft or more. The fragrant flower-heads appear between late spring and early autumn. Each waxy, star-shaped bloom is pale pink with a red centre. There are several varieties, including **variegata** (cream-edged leaves) and **exotica** (yellow-centred leaves). The dwarf **H. bella** is much more difficult to grow	Wax Plant	◐	◌	🌡	💧💧💧	💧
HYACINTHUS The Dutch or Common Hyacinth is the most popular of all indoor bulbs. The leafless flower stalks bear 30 or more crowded bell-like flowers with fragrance that can fill a room. Bulbs specially prepared for Christmas blooming should be planted in September — bulbs for January-March flowering are planted in October. Roman Hyacinths have smaller and less tightly-packed flowers	Hyacinth	▥	◌	🌡	💧💧	—
HYDRANGEA MACROPHYLLA Hydrangeas are usually bought in flower during spring or summer. With care the blooms (white, purple, blue, pink or red) will last for about 6 weeks indoors. Stand the pot outdoors after flowering and overwinter in a cold but frost-free room	Hydrangea	▥	◌	🌡	💧💧💧	—
HYPOCYRTA GLABRA The Clog Plant produces large numbers of orange flowers in summer which look like tiny goldfish. The erect or arching branches bear dark green, fleshy leaves. This plant needs careful watering and frequent misting	Clog Plant	▥	●	🌡	💧💧	💧
IMPATIENS Impatiens has long been a favourite on both sides of the Atlantic. With care this plant can be made to flower at almost any time of the year and until recently it was only the species which were grown, such as **I. holstii, I. sultani** and the red-leaved **I. petersiana**. These days it is more usual to grow one of the compact (6–12 in.) hybrids such as **Imp, Rosette** and **Zig-Zag**. The latest introductions are the multicoloured-leaved New Guinea Hybrids	Busy Lizzie	▥	◌	🌡	💧💧💧	💧
IXORA COCCINEA A glossy-leaved shrub which bears large flower-heads in white, yellow, salmon, pink or red throughout the summer months. This is not a plant for the novice — leaves and flower buds readily drop if conditions are not right	Flame of the Woods	◐	●	🌡	💧💧💧	💧
JACOBINIA CARNEA The flowers appear in late summer, each plume-like flower-head bearing numerous pink tubular blooms. Unfortunately the flowering period is short and the coarse-leaved shrub is unattractive when not in flower	King's Crown	▥	●	🌡	💧💧💧	💧
JASMINUM The most popular and easiest Jasmine to grow is **J. polyanthum**, the Pink Jasmine. The pink buds open in winter into clusters of fragrant starry white flowers. Cut back after flowering. The White Jasmine (**J. officinale grandiflora**) is rather similar but blooms in summer and autumn. **J. primulinum** flowers are yellow and odourless	Jasmine	◐	◌	🌡	💧💧💧	💧💧
KALANCHOE BLOSSFELDIANA A bushy plant which can be bought in flower at any time of the year, but is most popular as a Christmas gift plant. The large flower-heads of 20–50 blooms last for many weeks. The usual colour is red, but there are hybrids in white, yellow, orange and lilac. Dwarfs (6 in. high) such as **Tom Thumb** are now available	Flaming Katy	◐	○	🌡	💧💧💧	—
KOHLERIA ERIANTHA The leaves are red-edged and velvety — in spring or summer the red or orange tubular flowers appear. The mouth of each bloom is blotched or speckled — the favourite variety **Rongo** has a white-veined mouth	Kohleria	◐	●	🌡	💧💧	💧
LACHENALIA ALOIDES The pendent tubular flowers are borne on 1 ft spotted stalks in winter — yellow petals tinged with green and red. Attractive, but not popular as it cannot survive in a heated room. The variety **lutea** is all-yellow	Cape Cowslip	◐	◌	🌡	💧💧💧	—
LANTANA CAMARA When not in bloom this shrub is unimpressive with coarse wrinkled leaves and prickly stems. However, in summer it is eye-catching — the globular flower-heads change colour from pale yellow to dark red as the tiny flowers mature	Yellow Sage	☀	◌	🌡	💧💧💧	💧

HOYA CARNOSA VARIEGATA
Golden Wax Plant

HYDRANGEA MACROPHYLLA
Hydrangea

HYPOCYRTA GLABRA
Clog Plant

IMPATIENS HOLSTII
Busy Lizzie

IXORA COCCINEA
Flame of the Woods

PLANT DETAILS		HOUSE PLANT RECORD					Easy or difficult
Dimensions	Family group	Variety grown	Year of arrival	Supplier	Performance during the year		Easy or difficult
Flowers ½ in. across	Flowering House Plant						Moderately easy
Flower-heads 6–8 in. long	Temporary Pot Plant						Moderately easy
Flower-heads –8 in. across	Temporary Pot Plant						Moderately easy
Flowers 1 in. long	Flowering House Plant						Moderately difficult
Flowers –2 in. across	Flowering House Plant						Easy
Height 3–4 ft — Flower-heads 4 in. across	Flowering House Plant						Difficult
Flower-heads 5 in. long	Flowering House Plant						Moderately difficult
Flowers 1–1½ in. across	Flowering House Plant						Easy
Flowers ¼ in. across	Temporary Pot Plant						Easy
Height 1–1½ ft — Flowers 1–2 in. long	Flowering House Plant						Moderately difficult
Height 1 ft — Flowers 1 in. long	Temporary Pot Plant						Moderately easy
Flower-heads 1–2 in. across	Flowering House Plant						Moderately easy

VARIETIES

JACOBINIA CARNEA
King's Crown

JASMINUM POLYANTHUM
Pink Jasmine

KALANCHOE BLOSSFELDIANA
Flaming Katy

KOHLERIA ERIANTHA
Kohleria

LACHENALIA ALOIDES
Cape Cowslip

LANTANA CAMARA
Yellow Sage

FLOWERING PLANTS

Varieties

Varieties	Common name	Light	Air humidity	Warmth	Water: Growing period	Water: Resting period
LILIUM There is a host of Lilium varieties — with bowl-shaped, trumpet-shaped or turk's cap-shaped flowers. The most popular species is **L. longiflorum** — the Easter Lily. It grows 3 ft tall and the white 6 in. long trumpets are heavily scented. Bulbs are planted in autumn immediately after purchase	Lily					—
MANETTIA INFLATA In good light this plant will bloom for most of the year — the yellow-tipped red flowers are small but plentiful enough to almost cover the plant. The twining stems can be supported or left to trail	Firecracker Plant					
MYRTUS COMMUNIS Bowl-shaped blooms appear in large numbers in summer. White-petalled, gold-stamened and fragrant — the flowers are followed by purple berries. Shiny aromatic leaves make Myrtle attractive all year round	Myrtle					
NARCISSUS Some of the large-flowered types, such as **King Alfred**, are quite suitable for indoor cultivation, but perhaps the best group of all are the Tazettas which produce bunches of flowers on each stem at Christmas or early in the New Year. Plant bulbs between August and October	Narcissus or Daffodil					—
NERINE FLEXUOSA An uncommon plant — a cluster of wavy-petalled pink or white lily-like flowers are borne on 2 ft flower stalks in autumn. The narrow, strap-like leaves appear after the flowers. **N. sarniensis** is the Guernsey Lily	Nerine					
NERIUM OLEANDER Oleander is a spreading shrub that will grow about 6 ft tall. The fragrant blooms (white, pink, red or yellow) appear in summer and are borne in clusters above the willow-like foliage. Wood and sap are poisonous	Oleander					
NERTERA DEPRESSA Creeping stems and small leaves form a surface-hugging mat. In early summer tiny flowers appear and these are followed by glassy orange berries which cover the plant for months. Usually discarded when the display is over	Bead Plant					
ORCHID Several types will grow quite happily under ordinary room conditions, provided you remember that each type has its own special needs. The 'easy' ones for the living room are **Cymbidium**, **Coelogyne**, **Odontoglossum**, **Paphiopedilum** and **Vuylstekeara**. Seek advice from a book, catalogue or expert	Orchid					
PACHYSTACHYS LUTEA The cone-shaped flower-heads are made up of golden bracts with small white blooms peeping through. The oval leaves are prominently veined. The flowering season is a long one — from late spring until autumn. Prune in spring	Lollipop Plant					
PASSIFLORA CAERULEA The flowers of this plant look intricate and delicate, but there is nothing delicate about this robust and undemanding climber. Each flower is short-lived, but they continue to appear all summer long	Passion Flower					
PELARGONIUM The Common or Zonal Pelargonium is by far the most popular type. The flowers are ½–1½ in. across in white, pink, orange, red or purple. The rounded leaves usually have a horseshoe marking. With sun and rather dry compost the flowering season can last nearly all year round. The Regal Pelargonium has larger, frillier and more colourful flowers, but is less prolific. The Trailing or Ivy-leaved Pelargonium has trailing stems and is widely used in hanging baskets	Geranium					
PITTOSPORUM TOBIRA A flat-topped tree with dark healthy leaves for poor situations. In spring the branches are crowned with clusters of creamy, star-faced flowers. The fragrance is reminiscent of orange blossom	Mock Orange					

LILIUM LONGIFLORUM Easter Lily

MANETTIA INFLATA Firecracker Plant

MYRTUS COMMUNIS Myrtle

NERINE FLEXUOSA Nerine

NERIUM OLEANDER Oleander

NERTERA DEPRESSA Bead Plant

PLANT DETAILS		HOUSE PLANT RECORD					Easy or difficult
Dimensions	Family group	Variety grown	Year of arrival	Supplier	Performance during the year		
Height 2½–4 ft — Flowers 1–10 in. across	Temporary Pot Plant						Moderately easy
Flowers ¾ in. long	Flowering House Plant						Moderately easy
Height 2 ft — Flowers ¾ in. long	Flowering House Plant						Moderately easy
Flowers 5 in. across	Temporary Pot Plant						Moderately easy
Height 2 ft — Flowers in. across	Temporary Pot Plant						Moderately easy
Height 6 ft — Flowers in. across	Flowering House Plant						Moderately easy
Fruits ¼ in. across	Temporary Pot Plant						Moderately easy
Depends on the species	Flowering House Plant						Depends on the species
Flower-heads 5 in. long	Flowering House Plant						Moderately easy
Flowers 3 in. across	Flowering House Plant						Easy
Flowers ½–2½ in. across	Flowering House Plant						Easy
Flowers ½ in. across	Flowering House Plant						Moderately easy

ODONTOGLOSSUM GRANDE
Tiger Orchid

PACHYSTACHYS LUTEA
Lollipop Plant

PASSIFLORA CAERULEA
Passion Flower

PELARGONIUM HORTORUM
Geranium

PITTOSPORUM TOBIRA
Mock Orange

FLOWERING PLANTS

Varieties

Common name	CONDITIONS REQUIRED				
	Light	Air humidity	Warmth	Water: Growing period	Water: Resting period

PLUMBAGO AURICULATA
Grow as a trailer or tie it to supports as a climber. Clusters of sky blue flowers appear throughout summer and autumn. The vigorous stems will reach 3–4 ft — keep in check by pruning in winter
— Common name: **Cape Leadwort** | Light: partial shade | Air humidity: misting | Warmth: moderate | Growing: 3 drops | Resting: 1 drop

POINSETTIA
The Poinsettia (proper name **Euphorbia pulcherrima**) with its large, scarlet flower-heads is *the* indoor plant symbol of Christmas. It is no longer a difficult plant to grow — modern varieties are compact (1–1½ ft), bushy and with flower-heads which should last for 2–6 months. Red remains the favourite colour, but white and pink varieties are available
— Common name: **Poinsettia** | Light: partial shade | Air humidity: grey circle | Warmth: warm | Growing: 2 drops | Resting: —

PRIMULA
Primulas bear large numbers of flowers during the winter months. Two garden types are grown indoors — the Common Primrose (**P. acaulis**) and the larger Polyanthus (**P. variabilis**). **P. malacoides** (Fairy Primrose) is the most popular of the Temporary Pot Plant types — fragrant small flowers arranged in tiers. The flowers of **P. obconica** are larger but the leaves can cause a rash. **P. sinensis** has frilly-edged petals — **P. kewensis** is the only yellow pot plant variety. Some varieties can be kept until next winter — water sparingly in summer
— Common name: **Primula** | Light: sun | Air humidity: misting | Warmth: moderate | Growing: 3 drops | Resting: 1 drop

PUNICA GRANATUM NANA
The ordinary Pomegranate is not suitable for the living room but the Dwarf Pomegranate makes an excellent pot plant. The leaves are glossy and the bright red tubular flowers appear in summer. Bright orange fruits may develop, but they will not ripen. Leaves drop during the winter
— Common name: **Dwarf Pomegranate** | Light: partial shade | Air humidity: misting | Warmth: moderate | Growing: 3 drops | Resting: 2 drops

RECHSTEINERIA
The hooded, bright red flowers are borne horizontally at the top of the 1 ft stems. Summer is the flowering season — remove stems bearing faded blooms to prolong the flowering season. Needs the same conditions as its close relative Gloxinia
— Common name: **Cardinal Flower** | Light: partial shade | Air humidity: grey circle | Warmth: warm | Growing: 2 drops | Resting: —

ROCHEA COCCINEA
R. coccinea is bought in flower — a neat plant with tubular blooms. The species is red, but the varieties are more popular — **alba** (white) or **bicolor** (red and white). Each stem is clothed with ranks of triangular leathery leaves
— Common name: **Crassula** | Light: partial shade | Air humidity: white circle | Warmth: moderate | Growing: 3 drops | Resting: — (small drop)

ROSA
A Miniature Rose looks just like an ordinary garden variety scaled down to size — the same leaves, the same wide range of colours and flower-shapes, the same range of fragrance. They cannot be kept indoors all year round — transfer the pots outdoors from early autumn to midwinter. High humidity needed indoors
— Common name: **Miniature Rose** | Light: sun | Air humidity: grey circle | Warmth: moderate | Growing: 3 drops | Resting: 1 drop

RUELLIA MAKOYANA
An eye-catching plant which would be popular if it was not so demanding — the atmosphere must be warm and moist. The leaves on the weak stems are velvety and veined in silver — the deep pink flowers are long flared trumpets
— Common name: **Monkey Plant** | Light: partial shade | Air humidity: grey circle | Warmth: warm | Growing: 3 drops | Resting: 2 drops

SAINTPAULIA
African Violets first appeared for sale in the 1920s — today there are thousands of varieties with a bewildering assortment of flower forms and colours. The main attraction is the ability to flower at almost any time of the year and the compact size which means a pot can easily fit on the windowsill. Follow the rules in The House Plant Expert and the plants will produce several flushes each year. The large-leaved varieties with white, pink, purple, blue or red flowers remain the favourites, but these days there are also miniatures and blooms which are boldly edged or striped
— Common name: **African Violet** | Light: partial shade | Air humidity: grey circle | Warmth: moderate | Growing: 2 drops | Resting: 2 drops

SALPIGLOSSIS SINUATA
An outstanding pot plant, but you won't find it in the shops. Raise it from seed — sow in early spring or autumn. The large velvety trumpets are available in many colours — the petals are dark-veined
— Common name: **Painted Tongue** | Light: sun | Air humidity: misting | Warmth: moderate | Growing: 3 drops | Resting: —

SANCHEZIA NOBILIS
A larger but much less popular relative of Aphelandra. It is hard to grow under ordinary room conditions, as it needs moist air at all times. The yellow tubular flowers appear in early summer above the yellow-veined leaves
— Common name: **Sanchezia** | Light: partial shade | Air humidity: grey circle | Warmth: warm | Growing: 2 drops | Resting: 1 drop

POINSETTIA
(EUPHORBIA PULCHERRIMA)
Poinsettia

PRIMULA ACAULIS
Common Primrose

PUNICA GRANATUM NANA
Dwarf Pomegranate

RECHSTEINERIA CARDINALIS
Cardinal Flower

ROCHEA COCCINEA
Crassula

PLANT DETAILS		HOUSE PLANT RECORD					Easy or difficult
Dimensions	Family group	Variety grown	Year of arrival	Supplier	Performance during the year		
Flowers 1 in. across	Flowering House Plant						Moderately easy
Height 1–1½ ft — lower-heads 1 ft across	Temporary Pot Plant						Moderately easy
Flowers ½–1½ in. across	Temporary Pot Plant						Moderately easy
Height 3 ft — Flowers 1 in. across	Temporary Pot Plant						Moderately easy
Height 1 ft — Flowers 2 in. long	Temporary Pot Plant						Moderately difficult
Height 1–1½ ft — Flowers 1 in. long	Flowering House Plant Succulent						Moderately easy
Height 6–12 in. — Flowers ½–1½ in. across	Temporary Pot Plant						Moderately difficult
Height 2 ft — Flowers 1½ in. across	Flowering House Plant						Difficult
Flowers 1–1½ in. across	Flowering House Plant						Moderately easy
Flowers 2 in. across	Temporary Pot Plant						Moderately easy
Height 3 ft — Flowers 2 in. long	Flowering House Plant						Difficult

VARIETIES

ROSA CHINENSIS MINIMA
Miniature Rose

RUELLIA MAKOYANA
Monkey Plant

SAINTPAULIA IONANTHA
African Violet

SALPIGLOSSIS SINUATA
Painted Tongue

SANCHEZIA NOBILIS
Sanchezia

FLOWERING PLANTS

Varieties

Common name	Light	Air humidity	Warmth	Water: Growing period	Water: Resting period
SCHIZANTHUS HYBRIDA — Multicoloured, orchid-like flowers with a distinct yellow eye are borne above the ferny foliage. Sow the seeds in spring or autumn — keep the plants in a cool place. Pinch out tips to induce bushiness — discard after flowering *Poor Man's Orchid*	partial sun	misted	warm	● ● ●	—
SMITHIANTHA HYBRIDA — The pendent tubular flowers are a blend of yellow, orange and/or pink, appearing on long stalks in autumn. The leaves are mottled and velvety. An attractive pot plant which is much happier in the conservatory than in the living room *Temple Bells*	shade	humid	warm	● ●	—
SOLANUM — **S. capsicastrum** (Winter Cherry) is sold in vast quantities every Christmas. The orange or red berries above the dark green foliage provide a festive touch. The berries will last for months if the pot is stood on the windowsill of a cool room. Jerusalem Cherry (**S. pseudocapsicum**) has similar berries, but they are larger and poisonous. Solanum must be kept outdoors during the summer months *Solanum*	partial sun	misted	warm	● ● ●	●
SPARMANNIA AFRICANA — A tree-like plant for the larger room — it grows quickly and its large downy leaves contrast nicely with dark leathery ones like Ficus. In early spring the golden-centred flowers appear. Prune after blooming has finished *House Lime*	partial sun	misted	warm	● ● ●	●
SPATHIPHYLLUM — There are two types — the popular **S. wallisii** which grows about 1 ft high and the less hardy but much larger **S. Mauna Loa**. In spring the arum-like flowers appear on long stalks above the spear-shaped leaves. The flowers change from white to pale green with age *Peace Lily*	shade	humid	warm	● ●	●
STAPELIA VARIEGATA — The large, star-shaped flowers are borne in summer at the base of the fleshy, erect stems. The blooms are intricately patterned in brown and cream — the most distinctive feature is the offensive smell. **S. gigantea** (blooms 10–12 in. across) is odourless but more difficult to grow *Carrion Flower*	sun	dry	warm	● ●	●
STEPHANOTIS FLORIBUNDA — The stems can reach 10 ft or more, but they are usually twined around a wire hoop in the pot. The white flowers are star-shaped and heavily-scented, appearing in clusters throughout the summer months. Cut back once flowering is finished *Wax Flower*	shade	misted	warm	● ● ●	●
STRELITZIA REGINAE — Generally agreed to be the most spectacular of indoor plants, and surprisingly easy to grow if kept well-lit and cool in winter. Blooms appear after 4–6 years — plumed beauties in red, yellow and purple above the large paddle-shaped leaves *Bird of Paradise*	sun	misted	warm	● ● ●	●
STREPTOCARPUS HYBRIDA — Trumpet-shaped flowers appear in summer above the rosette of strap-shaped leaves. The blooms are white, blue, pink, purple or red with prominently-veined throats. **Constant Nymph** (lilac, veined violet) is the most popular variety *Cape Primrose*	shade	misted	warm	● ● ●	●
STREPTOSOLEN JAMESONII — A rambling, weak-stemmed shrub which belongs in the conservatory rather than in the living room. Its main feature is the large clusters of marmalade-coloured flowers borne at the tip of each branch in spring or summer *Marmalade Bush*	partial sun	misted	warm	● ●	● ●
THUNBERGIA ALATA — One of the best pot plants to choose for covering a large area quickly and for providing summer colour. Sow seeds or buy a plant in spring — the brown-throated flowers bear white, yellow or orange petals. The twining stems need some form of support — discard after flowering *Black-eyed Susan*	partial sun	misted	warm	● ● ●	—
TILLANDSIA — The two most popular flowering Tillandsias have grassy leaves. **T. lindenii** (Blue-flowered Torch) has a flattened flower-head of pink bracts. This large 9–12 in. long 'flower' bears small blue and white flowers between the bracts. **T. cyanea** has a green and more compact flower-head with flowers which are all-blue *Tillandsia*	shade	misted	warm	● ●	● ●

SCHIZANTHUS HYBRIDA
Poor Man's Orchid

SOLANUM CAPSICASTRUM
Winter Cherry

SPARMANNIA AFRICANA
House Lime

SPATHIPHYLLUM WALLISII
Peace Lily

STAPELIA VARIEGATA
Carrion Flower

| PLANT DETAILS | | HOUSE PLANT RECORD | | | | Easy or difficult |
Dimensions	Family group	Variety grown	Year of arrival	Supplier	Performance during the year	
Flowers 1 in. across	Temporary Pot Plant					Moderately easy
Flowers 2 in. long	Temporary Pot Plant					Difficult
Fruits ½ in. across	Temporary Pot Plant					Moderately easy
Height 4 ft — Flowers 1½ in. across	Flowering House Plant					Moderately easy
Flowers 3 in. long	Flowering House Plant					Moderately difficult
Flowers 2–3 in. across	Flowering House Plant — Succulent					Easy
Flowers 1 in. across	Flowering House Plant					Difficult
Height 3–4 ft — Flowers 6 in. across	Flowering House Plant					Moderately easy
Flowers 2 in. across	Flowering House Plant					Moderately difficult
Height 4–6 ft — Flowers 1 in. across	Flowering House Plant					Moderately difficult
Flowers 2 in. across	Temporary Pot Plant					Moderately easy
Depends on the species	Flowering House Plant — Bromeliad					Moderately easy

VARIETIES

STEPHANOTIS FLORIBUNDA
Wax Flower

STRELITZIA REGINAE
Bird of Paradise

STREPTOCARPUS HYBRIDA
Cape Primrose

THUNBERGIA ALATA
Black-eyed Susan

TILLANDSIA LINDENII
Blue-flowered Torch

FLOWERING PLANTS

Varieties

	Common name	CONDITIONS REQUIRED				
		Light	Air humidity	Warmth	Water: Growing period	Water: Resting period
TULIPA The most satisfactory Tulips to grow indoors are the compact hybrids classed as Single Earlies (one ring of petals) and Double Earlies (several rings of petals). Some Species Tulips are also excellent for indoors — varieties of **T. kaufmanniana** and **T. greigii** can be used. Plant in September and October for blooms in January to April. After flowering store bulbs for planting outdoors	Tulip					—
VALLOTA SPECIOSA An excellent plant for a sunny windowsill. Plant the 5 in. bulb in spring — the leaves are evergreen and the red, bell-like flowers are borne at the top of 1–2 ft flower stalks in late summer	Scarborough Lily					
VELTHEIMIA CAPENSIS An unusual but good choice for growing indoors as a change from Hyacinths or Tulips. Plant the bulb in autumn — about 3-4 months later the 1 ft flower stalk appears with about 60 small but long-lasting tubular flowers at the top	Forest Lily					—
VRIESEA The Vrieseas are typical Bromeliads with **V. splendens** (Flaming Sword) as the best-known species. The flower-heads are up to 2 ft long — bright red above the arching, smooth-edged leaves. There are a number of other Vrieseas available, including the giant **V. regina** and the compact ones like **V. minor** and the multicoloured **V. psittacina**	Vriesea					
ZANTEDESCHIA AETHIOPICA One of the real beauties of the indoor plant world. The upturned white trumpets are borne on 3 ft stalks in early spring above the fleshy, arrow-shaped leaves. The compost will need a daily soaking when the plant is actively growing	Calla Lily					—

TULIPA GREIGII
Tulip

VALLOTA SPECIOSA
Scarborough Lily

VELTHEIMIA CAPENSIS
Forest Lily

VRIESEA SPLENDENS
Flaming Sword

ZANTEDESCHIA AETHIOPICA
Calla Lily

PLANT DETAILS		HOUSE PLANT RECORD					Easy or difficult
Dimensions	Family group	Variety grown	Year of arrival	Supplier		Performance during the year	
Flowers 2–4 in. long	Temporary Pot Plant						Moderately easy
Height 1–2 ft — Flowers 3 in. across	Flowering House Plant						Easy
Height 1 ft — Flower-heads 4 in. long	Temporary Pot Plant						Moderately easy
Depends on the species	Flowering House Plant — Bromeliad						Moderately easy
Height 3 ft — Flowers 6–9 in. long	Temporary Pot Plant						Moderately easy

VARIETIES

CACTI

The cacti are a distinct family of succulents which originated on the American continent. All are leafless with the exception of Pereskia and young Opuntia. On the thickened stems there are small woolly patches (areoles) and in most cases outgrowths appear on these areoles — spines, needles, long hairs or short hooks. The cacti can live permanently under room conditions and many can be made to flower.

FOREST CACTI

The natural home is the forest regions of tropical America, where they live attached to the trunks of trees. Only a few varieties are commercially available, and most of them can be recognised by their trailing habit and their flattened leaf-like stems.

They may need watering and feeding in the winter months and some shade is required during the hottest months of the year. The Forest Cacti are suitable for north- and east-facing windowsills.

To help flowering provide a cool and dry resting period and never move the plant once buds appear. Allow the stems to harden outdoors during summer.

CONDITIONS REQUIRED				
Light	Air humidity	Warmth	Water: Growing period	Water: Resting period

Varieties	Common name	CACTUS RECORD: Year of arrival	CACTUS RECORD: Performance during the year
EPIPHYLLUM The Epiphyllums are untidy plants, the 2 ft long notched stems sprawling outwards unless staked when in flower. This unattractive growth habit is made up for by the flowers — flaring, multi-petalled trumpets which are 4–6 in. across. Nearly all are varieties of **E. ackermanii** — day-flowering plants available in a wide range of colours. The hybrids of **E. cooperi** are white, night-flowering and fragrant	Orchid Cactus		
RHIPSALIDOPSIS GAERTNERI The branching and arching stems are made up of flattened leaf-like 1½–2 in. long segments. It differs from Christmas Cactus by having scalloped-edged segments. The flowers are 1½ in. across — open bells of sharply-pointed petals. The colour range is pink to dark red and the flowering period is April and May	Easter Cactus		
RHIPSALIS CASSUTHA In its natural habitat this plant hangs from trees — indoors its long and branching pale green stems trail over the rim of the pot. Small summer flowers are followed by mistletoe-like fruits. It is not easy to find a supplier	Mistletoe Cactus		
RHIPSALIS PARADOXA The long stems are triangular and winged — at intervals they are narrowed to give a branched chain effect. It is a suitable plant for a hanging basket — white flowers appear in summer	Chain Cactus		
ZYGOCACTUS TRUNCATUS The branching and arching stems are made up of flattened leaf-like 1½–2 in. long segments. It differs from Easter Cactus by having toothed-edged segments. The flowers are 1 in. across — elongated with two tiers of swept-back petals. The colours include white, pink, red and purple, and the flowering period is mid November to late January	Christmas Cactus		

EPIPHYLLUM ACKERMANII
Orchid Cactus

RHIPSALIDOPSIS GAERTNERI
Easter Cactus

RHIPSALIS CASSUTHA
Mistletoe Cactus

RHIPSALIS PARADOXA
Chain Cactus

ZYGOCACTUS TRUNCATUS
Christmas Cactus

DESERT CACTI

The natural home is the warm semi-desert regions of America. Despite the name of the group very few can exist in sand alone. Nearly all cacti belong here and there are hundreds to choose from. Most types are easily propagated from cuttings.

They need very little water between mid autumn and early spring and they require as much sunshine as possible, especially for flowering. The Desert Cacti are suitable for south-facing windowsills.

To help flowering provide cool, sunny and almost dry conditions in winter and then a boost to growth in summer — regular watering with tepid water, lots of sunshine and plenty of fresh air. Keep the plant slightly pot-bound.

CONDITIONS REQUIRED				
Light	Air humidity	Warmth	Water: Growing period	Water: Resting period
☀	○	🌡	💧💧	💧

Varieties

Varieties	Common name	CACTUS RECORD	
		Year of arrival	Performance during the year
APOROCACTUS FLAGELLIFORMIS A popular and easy cactus. The brown-spined slender stems droop over the rim of the pot — quick-growing, adding several inches each year. The 3 in. long pink and tubular flowers appear in spring — the flowering season lasts for 7–10 weeks	Rat's Tail Cactus		
ASTROPHYTUM The Astrophytums begin life as prominently-ribbed balls but become cylindrical with age. **A. capricorne** (Goat's Horn Cactus) has curved spines, **A. ornatum** (Star Cactus) bears long straight spines and **A. myriostigma** (Bishop's Cap) has no spines at all. Yellow daisy-like flowers are produced in summer on mature plants	Astrophytum		
CEPHALOCEREUS SENILIS The grey-green columnar stem grows slowly, putting on less than 1 in. per year. This stem is covered by 5 in. long silvery hairs — hence the common name. Mature height is 1 ft — it does not flower indoors	Old Man Cactus		
CEREUS PERUVIANUS A common sight in any cactus collection — columnar stems with prominent ribs and regular clusters of brown spines along each rib. Stems reach 2–3 ft in time and bear 6 in. long flowers in summer. The variety **monstrosus** bears distorted stems with irregular ribs	Column Cactus		
CHAMAECEREUS SILVESTRII The Peanut Cactus is an old favourite for two reasons. Firstly it spreads rapidly, its white-spined, finger-like stems soon covering the top of the compost. It also flowers readily, the 2½ in. long funnel-shaped flowers appearing in spring. The colour is orange-scarlet	Peanut Cactus		
CLEISTOCACTUS STRAUSSII In time this slow-growing columnar cactus will reach 4 ft. There are many ribs on the slender stems and it is covered with fine white bristles and wool, giving the plant a silvery appearance	Silver Torch Cactus		
ECHINOCACTUS GRUSONII A slow-growing ribbed ball — it takes 10 years to reach a diameter of 6–9 in. There is a golden crown of woolly hairs at the top and there are prominent golden spines along the ribs. It will not flower indoors	Barrel Cactus		
ECHINOCEREUS There are several species, ranging from globular to distinctly cylindrical. The popular column-like one with numerous ribs and comb-like spines is **E. pectinatus** (Hedgehog Cactus). The smaller **E. knippelianus** is more ball-like and less spiny	Echinocereus		

VARIETIES

APOROCACTUS FLAGELLIFORMIS
Rat's Tail Cactus

ASTROPHYTUM CAPRICORNE
Goat's Horn Cactus

CEPHALOCEREUS SENILIS
Old Man Cactus

CEREUS PERUVIANUS
Column Cactus

CHAMAECEREUS SILVESTRII
Peanut Cactus

ECHINOCACTUS GRUSONII
Barrel Cactus

DESERT CACTI

Varieties

	Common name	CACTUS RECORD	
		Year of arrival	Performance during the year
ECHINOFOSSULOCACTUS ZACATECASENSIS A terrible name — fortunately it is usually sold as **Stenocactus**. The stem is a 6 in. globe with wavy ribs and long spines. The upper areoles are white and densely woolly. Flowers are white tipped with pink and 1½ in. across	Brain Cactus		
ECHINOPSIS EYRIESII A globular or short columnar stem with short spines. Nothing special, but in summer the 6 in. long flowers appear — white, multi-petalled and fragrant. A larger species (**E. rhodotricha**) bears 1 in. spines and scentless flowers	Sea Urchin Cactus		
ESPOSTOA LANATA A 1–2 ft column with a dense covering of silky white hairs through which the sharp spines protrude. Unlike Cleistocactus this one does not bloom indoors. The hairs of the closely related **E. melanostele** turn black with age	Snowball Cactus		
FEROCACTUS LATISPINUS A fearsome plant — the grey-green barrel-shaped stem has prominent ribs which bear red spines which are large and hooked. This cactus rarely blooms indoors	Fish Hook Cactus		
GYMNOCALYCIUM MIHANOVICHII Most species and varieties of Gymnocalycium are rather ordinary, but there is one group of these small ball-like cacti which are entirely red or yellow. These strains of **G. mihanovichii friedrichii** lack chlorophyll and so are grafted on to a green cactus	Red Cap Cactus		
HAMATOCACTUS SETISPINUS At first sight this globular or short columnar cactus can be mistaken for Ferocactus. There are prominent ribs and the spines are large and hooked. But here the ribs are curved and notched, and yellow blooms are produced each summer	Strawberry Cactus		
LEMAIREOCEREUS MARGINATUS Much branched in nature, but in the home it is a single column with prominent ribs. Similar in general form to Cereus, but with the Organ Pipe Cactus the areoles bear dense white wool and a white line is formed along each rib	Organ Pipe Cactus		
LOBIVIA A good cactus for the beginner — it remains compact (3–6 in. high) and readily produces red or yellow flowers. **L. aurea** (Golden Lily Cactus) is ball-shaped — **L. famatimensis** (Sunset Cactus) is columnar with many ribs and yellow spines	Lobivia		
MAMMILLARIA BOCASANA Mammillarias are popular because they are small and they flower even when quite young. The key recognition feature it shares with Rebutia is the presence of cluster-forming stems which bear spine-topped tubercles in place of ribs. The favourite species is **M. bocasana**, a silvery plant with a ring of small white blooms around the stem in spring	Powder Puff Cactus		
MYRTILLOCACTUS GEOMETRIZANS An unusual cactus which is worth adding to a collection. It is a columnar tree type — the stem produces several branches and the surface turns blue with age. The ribs bear long spines	Blue Myrtle Cactus		
NOTOCACTUS Despite the common name some species become oval or cylindrical with age. **N. ottonis** is a typical Notocactus — spherical, fiercely-spined and bearing large yellow flowers on plants which are only a few years old. **N. leninghausii** is a columnar type grown for its densely-spined stems rather than for its blooms	Ball Cactus		

ESPOSTOA LANATA Snowball Cactus

FEROCACTUS LATISPINUS Fish Hook Cactus

GYMNOCALYCIUM MIHANOVICHII FRIEDRICHII Red Cap Cactus

LEMAIREOCEREUS MARGINATUS Organ Pipe Cactus

MAMMILLARIA BOCASANA Powder Puff Cactus

NOTOCACTUS OTTONIS Ball Cactus

DESERT CACTI

Varieties

	Common name	CACTUS RECORD	
		Year of arrival	Performance during the year
OPUNTIA Opuntias come in all sizes ranging from tiny prostrate plants to towering trees. The popular ones bear flattened pads and are the Prickly Pears of tropical regions. It does not flower indoors. The favourite one is **O. microdasys** which grows about 1 ft high. It bears tiny golden barbs — these are white on the variety **albinospina** and red on **O. rufida**	Prickly Pear		
OREOCEREUS CELSIANUS An oval cactus with white hairs and a woolly top — hence the common name. With age the yellow spines turn red, branches arise from the base and 3 in. long red flowers appear. **O. trollii** is smaller and bears fewer ribs	Old Man of the Andes		
PARODIA SANGUINIFLORA Rather like Mammillaria but they are usually solitary plants which do not readily form offsets at the base. The popular red-flowering Parodia is **P. sanguiniflora** — the yellow-flowering types are **P. aureispina** and **P. chrysacanthion**	Tom Thumb Cactus		
PERESKIA This one looks nothing like a cactus — it is a semi-evergreen shrub with spiny stems and 3 in. long leaves. The flowers look like wild roses — hence the common name. The popular one is the green-leaved **P. aculeata** which reaches 6 ft. The golden-leaved **P. godseffiana** is more attractive	Rose Cactus		
REBUTIA MINISCULA Like Mammillaria and Parodia this cactus is a popular compact plant with tubercles rather than ribs. The bright trumpet-shaped flowers are borne close to the base rather than forming a ring around the top as occurs with the Mammillarias. **R. miniscula** is the favourite one — 2 in. balls with orange, red or violet flowers in early summer	Mexican Sunball		
TRICHOCEREUS This cactus is grown for its tall columnar stems — **T. spachianus** forms an impressive bristly column about 5 ft tall. The smaller **T. candicans** branches freely and bears large areoles with long yellow spines. Huge white flowers are borne on mature plants	Torch Cactus		

OPUNTIA BERGERIANA
Opuntia

OPUNTIA MICRODASYS
Bunny Ears

OREOCEREUS CELSIANUS
Old Man of the Andes

PARODIA SANGUINIFLORA
Tom Thumb Cactus

REBUTIA MINISCULA
Mexican Sunball

TRICHOCEREUS CANDICANS
Torch Cactus

CHAPTER 3
CARE

Suppliers

Name	Comments
Local	
Mail Order	

BUYING PLANTS

Take care when buying plants in winter. Plants stood outside will have been damaged by the cold unless they are hardy varieties.

Bad Signs

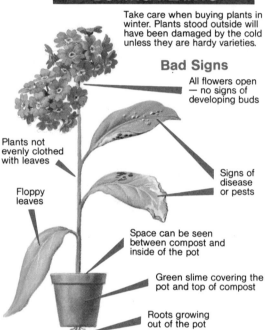

All flowers open — no signs of developing buds

Signs of disease or pests

Plants not evenly clothed with leaves

Floppy leaves

Space can be seen between compost and inside of the pot

Green slime covering the pot and top of compost

Roots growing out of the pot

TAKING PLANTS HOME

The plant should be properly wrapped before it is taken out of the shop or garden centre. There are two reasons for this action — the wrapping will protect stray leaves from damage and it will also keep out cold draughts. In winter the protective cover should be closed at the top.

The danger of walking home with a delicate house plant in the depths of winter is obvious — less obvious is the damage which can result from putting a plant in the boot of a car in the height of summer. Plants can be killed by baking as well as by freezing. When taking a plant home by car the best plan is to secure it in a box and place it on a seat.

THE SETTLING-IN PERIOD

In most cases the plant you have bought will need a period of acclimatisation in its new home — this is the settling-in period. For a few weeks keep it out of direct sunlight and draughts, and be careful not to give it too much heat or water. It is quite normal for a delicate variety to lose a leaf or two during the settling-in period, and the worst thing you can do is to keep moving it from one spot to another in order to find the 'proper' home. Just leave it alone in a draught-free reasonably bright spot.

Temporary Pot Plants (e.g Azalea, Chrysanthemum and Cyclamen) which are purchased in flower during the winter months require different treatment — put them in their chosen quarters immediately and provide as much light as possible.

BUYING OTHER THINGS

Shown here are the essentials you will require. There are many additional aids which can be bought by the keen house plant grower. A maximum-minimum thermometer and a hygrometer will reveal temperature and humidity around the plants. A propagating frame is a useful piece of equipment for rooting difficult cuttings and a range of pot covers should be bought for hiding unsightly pots.

POTS

The basic pot is made of clay or plastic. Each type has its own group of devotees, but both sorts will support perfectly good plants. The most useful sizes are 2½, 3½, 5 and 7 in. pots — keep a supply handy together with the appropriate-sized drip saucers which are necessary for catching drainage water.

✓ when bought

COMPOST

Ordinary soil should never be used for potting house plants — a sterile compost should be purchased. Most people prefer a peat-based one rather than a soil compost. The compost is used for repotting and taking cuttings — you can buy specific types for each of these jobs but it is easier to rely on a multipurpose brand.

✓ when bought

MISTER

A mister is a small-capacity hand-generated sprayer with a nozzle capable of producing a mist-like spray. It performs two vital functions. Used with plain water it deposits a coating of small droplets on the leaves — this is a routine treatment for plants which need high humidity. When pests or disease are present the recommended quantity of pesticide is added to the water and the leaves are then sprayed as directed on the label.

✓ when bought

WATERING CAN

Take care when choosing a watering can. Its capacity should be 2–6 pints and the spout should be long and also narrow at the opening. A detachable fine rose is a useful extra. For the really keen there are pump-action waterers for hanging baskets and tap-attached mini-hoses for watering large numbers of house plants.

✓ when bought

FERTILIZER

All plants, indoors and out, need an adequate supply of nitrogen, phosphates and potash together with small amounts of trace elements. The soil or compost in the pot contains a limited amount of food, and this is soon depleted by the roots of the plant and by leaching through the drainage holes. Thus regular feeding when the plant is actively growing must take place. A liquid feed such as Baby Bio is the most popular way of adding the necessary plant nutrients to the compost.

✓ when bought

STAKES, STRING & SECATEURS

Pruning and training are essential features of good house plant care. You will need supports for climbing plants — canes, stakes, trellises, moss sticks etc are available. Avoid single canes where possible — use a framework of three or four stakes. String or proprietary ties are necessary for attaching the stems — do not tie too tightly. Secateurs are required for pruning, and dead-heading faded flowers. Buy a narrow-bladed pair — do not choose the blade-and-anvil type.

✓ when bought

FIRST-AID KIT

Nobody wants a kitchen filled with a large collection of bottles, boxes and assorted brews. It is, however, a good idea to keep a small plant-aid kit for emergency use. You will need a bottle of insecticide recommended for indoor use to deal with a greenfly or whitefly attack — you will also need a systemic fungicide to prevent the spread of botrytis and powdery mildew. Always follow the maker's instructions — read page 58.

✓ when bought

THE HOUSE PLANT EXPERT

For many years THE HOUSE PLANT EXPERT has been the bible for millions of indoor gardeners, and is now the best-selling house plant book in the world. This volume covers the same varieties, but The House Plant Expert has many additional features. For each variety the Secrets of Success are clearly spelt out, and the Special Problems of the popular types are listed. Unusual as well as common problems are illustrated and described, and so are all the methods of propagation.

✓ when bought

CARE

WATER

More plants die through overwatering than any other single cause — they are killed by kindness. Roots need air as well as water, which means that the compost should be moist but not saturated. Some plants need a partial drying-out period between waterings, others do not. The correct frequency of water is not a constant feature — Busy Lizzie may need watering daily in summer and Bishop's Cap may not need watering all winter.

First of all, you must think about the environment. As the temperature and light intensity increase, so does the need for water. Plants in small pots need more frequent watering — so do those in clay pots compared with those in plastic ones. Next there is the season to consider — in winter watering one to three times a month is usually sufficient for foliage plants during this resting season.

Tap water is suitable for nearly all plants, but for delicate varieties you should allow it to stand overnight to get rid of some of the chlorine and to let it reach room temperature. Hard water can be harmful to lime-hating plants which are permanent residents indoors, but for short-term residents (e.g Azalea, Erica) the use of hard water will not pose a problem.

Plants which do not like water on their leaves (Saintpaulia, Gloxinia, Cyclamen etc) should be watered by the Immersion Method. For other plants use the Watering Can Method and occasionally use the Immersion Method where practical.

Watering Can Method

Never water in full sun — leaves may be scorched.
In winter water in the morning if the room is unheated

① Insert spout **under** the leaves — pour water steadily and gently. In summer fill the space to the top of the pot — in winter stop as soon as water begins to drain

② Empty after 30 minutes

Immersion Method

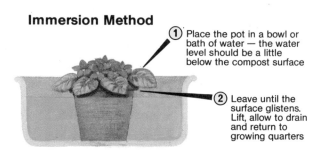

① Place the pot in a bowl or bath of water — the water level should be a little below the compost surface

② Leave until the surface glistens. Lift, allow to drain and return to growing quarters

Watering Guide

DRY IN WINTER Plants Desert Cacti and Succulents should be treated as Moist/Dry Plants during the active growth season from spring to autumn. During the winter the compost should be allowed to dry out almost completely.

MOIST/DRY Plants Most foliage house plants belong in this group. The standard recommendation is to water thoroughly and frequently between spring and autumn, and to water sparingly in winter, letting the top ½ in. of compost dry out each time between waterings. This drying out of the surface between waterings is especially important during the resting period from late October to March.

MOIST AT ALL TIMES Plants Most flowering plants belong in this group. The compost is kept moist, *but not wet*, at all times. The standard recommendation is to water carefully each time the surface becomes dry, but never frequently enough to keep the compost permanently saturated. There is no rule to tell you which plant belongs here — check the label or The House Plant Expert.

WET AT ALL TIMES Plants Very few plants belong in this group. Water thoroughly and frequently enough to keep the compost wet, not merely moist. Examples are Acorus, Azalea and Cyperus.

Watering Problems

Cause ▶	Too little water	Too much water	Surface caking	Compost shrinkage away from pot
Effects ▶	Leaves limp and wilted — little or no growth	Leaves limp with rotten areas — little growth	Water not absorbed. Prick over the surface with a fork or small trowel, then water by the Immersion Method. Future waterings can be by the Watering Can Method	Water runs straight through. Water by the Immersion Method — do not remove the pot until the compost touches the sides. Future waterings can be by the Watering Can Method
	Lower leaves curled and yellow — edges brown	Lower leaves curled and yellow — tips brown		
	Oldest leaves fall first	Young and old leaves fall at the same time		
	Flowers fade or fall	Flowers mouldy		
	Roots dry	Roots mushy		

LIGHT

The **intensity** of light required for satisfactory growth varies enormously from plant to plant. Some types will flourish on a sunny windowsill but quickly deteriorate in a shady corner — Pelargoniums and Miniature Roses are good examples. At the other extreme there are many plants such as Fittonia and Pellionia which flourish in light shade but cannot survive exposure to sunlight. Finally there are the cast-iron plants like Chlorophytum which will grow in either sun or shade. The appropriate pages of this book will give you an indication of the light intensity required — page 2 provides a list of plants for various light conditions. Use distance from the window (see below) rather than your eye to judge light intensity. You may notice little difference when moving from the window to about 4 ft within the room, but the light intensity will have dropped by about 95 per cent.

Light **duration** is a different concept and does not vary greatly from plant to plant. Nearly all types need 12–16 hours per day of either natural light or sufficiently strong artificial illumination in order to maintain active growth. Less light than this results in a slowing down of food production.

Artificial light allows you to supplement the duration and intensity of natural light in winter so that the plants remain in active growth — Saintpaulias can be kept in bloom almost all year round. Use a fitting with 2 x 40 watts Gro-Lux tubes — place them 6–12 in. above flowering plants or 12–24 in. above foliage plants.

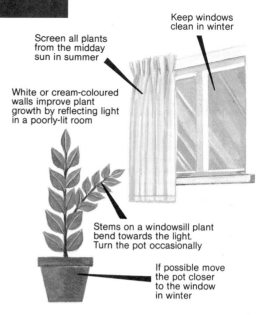

Keep windows clean in winter

Screen all plants from the midday sun in summer

White or cream-coloured walls improve plant growth by reflecting light in a poorly-lit room

Stems on a windowsill plant bend towards the light. Turn the pot occasionally

If possible move the pot closer to the window in winter

CARE

Light Guide — see page 2 for a list of examples

▲ **DEEP SHADE**
Unsuitable for all indoor plants.

▲ **SHADE**
Poorly-lit area, but bright enough to allow you to read a newspaper during several hours of the day. Few foliage plants will actually flourish here — Aglaonema, Aspidistra and Asplenium are exceptions. Many Semi-Shade plants, however, will adapt and are capable of surviving in the darker conditions. No flowering plants are suitable.

▲ **SEMI-SHADE**
Moderately-lit area, within 5–8 ft of a sunlit window or close to a sunless window
Very few flowering plants will flourish in this part of the room, but many foliage house plants will grow quite happily here. Most of the Bright but Sunless foliage plants will adapt to these conditions.

▲ **BRIGHT BUT SUNLESS**
Area close to but not in the zone lit by direct sunlight
Many plants grow best when placed in this region which extends for about 5 ft around a window which is sunlit for part of the day. A large sunless windowsill may provide similar conditions.

▲ **SOME DIRECT SUN**
Brightly-lit area, with some sunlight falling on the leaves during the day
Examples are a west-facing or an east-facing windowsill, a spot close to but more than 2 ft away from a south-facing windowsill or on a south-facing windowsill which is partly obstructed. This is the ideal site for many flowering and some foliage house plants.

▲ **FULL SUN**
Area with as much light as possible, within 2 ft of a south-facing window
Very few house plants can withstand scorching conditions — only the Desert Cacti, Succulents and Pelargonium can be expected to flourish in unshaded continuous sunshine during the summer months. By providing light shade at midday during hot weather a much larger list can be grown.

Light Problems

Cause ▶	Too little light	Too much light	Movement from shade to sun	Movement from sun to shade
Effects ▶	Growth spindly or absent — leaves smaller and paler than normal	Leaves have a 'washed-out' appearance — brown or grey scorch marks present	Scorch marks appear on leaves — growth is slowed down and leaves may fall. Never move a plant from a shady spot to a sunny windowsill or the open garden. Acclimatise it for a few days by moving it to a brighter spot each day	No dramatic symptoms with a foliage plant — it will survive but not flourish and it may slowly deteriorate. Try to move it back to normal light requirements for a week every 1–2 months. Flowering plants are more seriously affected — the floral display is bound to disappoint
	Lower leaves turn yellow, then dry up and fall	Leaves wilt at midday — with 'sun-shy' varieties leaves shrivel and die		
	Blooms poor or absent in flowering types			

HUMIDITY

House plants need less warm air and more moist air than you think — papery leaves generally need more humidity in the air than thick, leathery ones.

Cold air requires only a small amount of water vapour before it becomes saturated, and so on an average winter day the air is moist. When you turn on a radiator, the capacity of the surrounding air to hold water vapour is greatly increased. As the room becomes comfortable the amount of water vapour in the air is no longer enough to keep it moist.

If you wish to grow more than the dry-air plants listed on page 2 in a centrally-heated room, you will have to use a humidifying technique. You can try a humidifier to increase the moisture content of the whole room, but it is more usual to use one or more of the techniques which produce a moist microclimate around each plant.

You can use a mister to deposit a coating of fine droplets over the leaves. Use tepid water, and treat plants in a cool room in the morning. Cover all the plant and not just one side. Do not mist when the leaves are exposed to bright sunlight.

Grouping plants together is another technique for increasing the moisture in the microclimate. The best method of increasing the humidity in this way is to use a Pebble Tray — see page 4.

Double potting is still another technique. Use an outer waterproof container and fill the space between it and the pot with moist peat. Keep this peat thoroughly and continually damp.

Humidity Guide

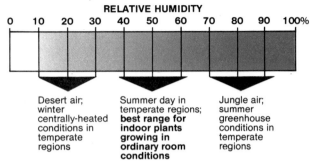

RELATIVE HUMIDITY

0 10 20 30 40 50 60 70 80 90 100%

Desert air; winter centrally-heated conditions in temperate regions

Summer day in temperate regions; **best range for indoor plants growing in ordinary room conditions**

Jungle air; summer greenhouse conditions in temperate regions

Humidity Problems

Cause ▶	Too little humidity	Too much humidity
Effects	Leaf tips brown and shrivelled	Leaf surface covered with grey mould
	Leaf edges yellow — wilting may occur	Leaves and stem rotten — Cacti and Succulents are very sensitive
	Buds and flowers shrivel and fall	Buds and flowers covered with grey mould

WARMTH

Nearly all indoor plants will flourish if the temperature is kept within the 55°–75°F range — most types will grow quite happily in rooms which are a little too cool for human comfort. There are exceptions to this general rule. Some flowering pot plants and a few foliage plants need much cooler conditions than the human comfort zone — a maximum winter temperature of 60°F is required. At the other end of the scale the tender varieties require conditions which never fall below 60°F.

Most plants are quite tolerant and can survive temperatures which for a short time are above or below the stated range. The real enemy is temperature fluctuation. As a general rule plants appreciate a drop of 5°–10°F at night but a sudden cooling down of 20°F can be damaging or fatal. Cacti and Succulents are the exceptions — they thrive on hot days and cold nights.

Temperature Problems

Cause ▶	Too little warmth	Too much warmth
Effects ▶	Leaves curl	Leaves wilt
	Brown patches or edges appear	Brown tips or edges appear
	Young or old leaves fall	Oldest leaves fall
		Flowers quickly fade
		Spindly growth occurs during the resting season if light is good

Temperature Guide — see Varieties (pages 6—49) for examples

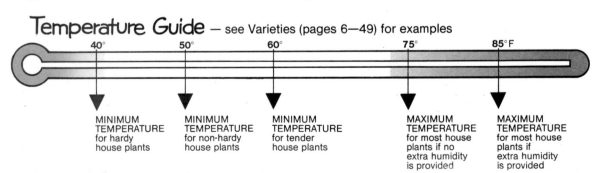

40° 50° 60° 75° 85°F

MINIMUM TEMPERATURE for hardy house plants

MINIMUM TEMPERATURE for non-hardy house plants

MINIMUM TEMPERATURE for tender house plants

MAXIMUM TEMPERATURE for most house plants if no extra humidity is provided

MAXIMUM TEMPERATURE for most house plants if extra humidity is provided

FEEDING

The soil or peat compost in the pot contains a strictly limited amount of food, and this reservoir of nutrients is continually depleted by the roots of the plant and by leaching through the drainage holes. Potting compost contains enough plant food for about two months after repotting. Once this nutrient supply has been exhausted it is necessary to apply a fertilizer if the plant is not dormant. Cacti can survive for a long time without any feeding, but vigorous foliage plants and flowering plants coming into bloom will be seriously affected if not fed regularly.

The time for this regular feeding is during the growing and flowering seasons — March to October for foliage and most flowering plants, and during November to January for winter-flowering types. Feeding should be reduced or stopped during the resting period.

A wide range of house plant fertilizers is available. Powder and granules are widely used outdoors but have only a limited use for house plants. The insoluble material does not readily travel down to the roots and you cannot cut off the food supply once the resting season arrives. The same problem applies to pills and sticks, which can also promote one-sided root development.

The most popular way to feed pot plants is to use a liquid fertilizer such as Baby Bio. Watering and feeding are carried out in one operation, which means that there is no danger of overfeeding as the food is applied little and often.

Feeding Guide

Use a compound fertilizer containing nitrogen, phosphates and potash. If there is no statement for one of them on the label then you can be sure it is missing.		
NITROGEN (N)	**The leaf maker** which promotes stem growth and foliage production. Needs to be balanced with some potash for flowering plants	
PHOSPHATES (P_2O_5)	**The root maker** which stimulates active rooting in the compost. Necessary for both foliage and flowering types	
POTASH (K_2O)	**The flower maker** which hardens growth so that flowering and fruiting are encouraged at the expense of leaf growth	
TRACE ELEMENTS	Present in some house plant foods — derived from humus extracts or added chemicals. Shortage can result in discoloured leaves	

Feeding Problems

Cause ▶	Too little fertilizer	Too much fertilizer
Effects ▶	Slow growth — little resistance to pests and diseases	Lanky and weak growth in winter — abnormal growth in summer
	Leaves pale with 'washed-out' appearance. Lower leaves drop — weak stems	Leaves wilted with scorched edges and brown spots
	Flowers absent or small and poorly coloured	Excessive leaf production may mask floral display

CARE

RESTING

Nearly all indoor plants need a dormant or resting period during the year, and this generally takes place in winter. Some plants give unmistakable signs that they are at the end of their growing period and it is obvious that the usual maintenance routine has to change. The top growth of bulbs (e.g Hyacinth) dies down and the leaves of deciduous plants (e.g Rosa) turn brown and fall.

Evergreen house plants may give little or no indication that the resting period has arrived. But as midwinter approaches the duration of natural light is too short to support active growth. This means that you must reduce the frequency of watering and feeding. The appearance of new growth in the spring is a sure sign that the resting period is over. Slowly resume normal watering and feeding and repot the plant if necessary.

Winter-flowering plants are an exception — feed and water regularly whilst the display lasts.

CLEANING

Dust creates a number of problems. The obvious effect is to spoil the appearance of the plant — less obvious are the blocking of the breathing pores, the screening out of daylight and the possibility of a harmful chemical action on the leaves.

Remove dust before it becomes unsightly. Syringe or sponge the leaves with clean water — do this job in the morning so that the foliage will be dry before nightfall. When the leaves are very dirty they should be lightly dusted before washing. Support leaves when cleaning and for hairy- or spiny-leaved plants it is better to use a soft dry brush rather than water.

Foliage, even when clean, tends to become dull with age. Many plant-polishing materials are available, but you must choose with care. Olive oil produces a shine but it also collects dust — it is better to buy a proprietary product and follow the instructions carefully.

TAKING CUTTINGS

The chance of success depends on the variety — some woody plants are difficult or impossible to propagate without special equipment, whereas cuttings of some popular plants such as Hedera, Tradescantia and Impatiens will form roots in a glass of water.

As a general rule early summer is the best time for rooting cuttings, although late summer is the popular time for Fuchsia and Pelargonium cuttings.

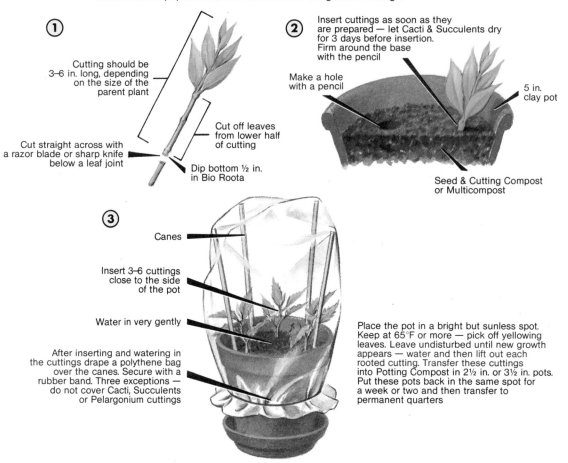

①

Cutting should be 3–6 in. long, depending on the size of the parent plant

Cut off leaves from lower half of cutting

Cut straight across with a razor blade or sharp knife below a leaf joint

Dip bottom ½ in. in Bio Roota

② Insert cuttings as soon as they are prepared — let Cacti & Succulents dry for 3 days before insertion. Firm around the base with the pencil

Make a hole with a pencil

5 in. clay pot

Seed & Cutting Compost or Multicompost

③

Canes

Insert 3–6 cuttings close to the side of the pot

Water in very gently

After inserting and watering in the cuttings drape a polythene bag over the canes. Secure with a rubber band. Three exceptions — do not cover Cacti, Succulents or Pelargonium cuttings

Place the pot in a bright but sunless spot. Keep at 65°F or more — pick off yellowing leaves. Leave undisturbed until new growth appears — water and then lift out each rooted cutting. Transfer these cuttings into Potting Compost in 2½ in. or 3½ in. pots. Put these pots back in the same spot for a week or two and then transfer to permanent quarters

Cuttings Record

Date	Variety	Results

CULTURAL PROBLEMS

PLANT GROWING SLOWLY OR NOT AT ALL In winter this is normal for nearly all plants, so do not force it to grow. In summer the most likely cause is UNDERFEEDING, OVERWATERING or TOO LITTLE LIGHT. If these factors are not responsible, and the temperature is in the recommended range, then the plant is probably POT-BOUND.

UPPER LEAVES FIRM BUT YELLOW This is generally due to the use of CALCIUM in the compost of lime-hating plants or the use of HARD WATER for watering such plants.

SPOTS OR PATCHES ON LEAVES If spots or patches are crisp and brown, UNDERWATERING is the most likely cause. If the areas are soft and dark brown, OVERWATERING is the probable reason. If spots or patches are white or straw-coloured, the trouble is due to WATERING WITH COLD WATER, WATER SPLASHES ON LEAVES, AEROSOL DAMAGE, TOO MUCH SUN or PEST/DISEASE DAMAGE. If spots are moist and blister-like or dry and sunken, the cause is DISEASE. Several PESTS can cause speckling of the leaf surface.

LEAVES CURL AND FALL Curling followed by leaf fall is a sign of TOO LITTLE HEAT, OVERWATERING or COLD DRAUGHTS.

SUDDEN LEAF FALL Rapid defoliation without a prolonged preliminary period of wilting or discolouration is generally due to a SHOCK to the plant's system. There may have been a large drop or rise in temperature, a sudden increase in daytime light intensity or an intense cold draught. DRYNESS at the roots below the critical level can result in this sudden loss of leaves, especially with woody specimens.

FLOWER BUDS FALL The conditions which cause leaf drop can also lead to loss of buds and flowers. The commonest causes are DRY AIR, UNDERWATERING, TOO LITTLE LIGHT, MOVING THE POT and INSECT DAMAGE.

VARIEGATED LEAVES TURN ALL-GREEN The simple explanation here is that the foliage is not receiving sufficient light. Remove the all-green branch (if practical) and move the pot closer to the window.

ROTTING LEAVES AND STEMS This is due to disease attack where growing conditions are poor. The fault often lies with OVERWATERING in winter or LEAVING WATER ON LEAVES at night.

LOWER LEAVES TURN YELLOW AND FALL It is quite normal for an occasional lower leaf on a mature plant to turn yellow and eventually fall. When several leaves turn yellow at the same time and then fall, the most likely cause is OVERWATERING or COLD DRAUGHTS.

GREEN SLIME ON CLAY POT A sure sign of watering problems — OVERWATERING or BLOCKED DRAINAGE is the cause.

SMALL, PALE LEAVES; SPINDLY GROWTH This occurs in winter and early spring when the plant has been kept too warm and the compost too wet for the limited amount of light available. Where practical, prune off this poor quality growth. If these symptoms appear in the growing season, the most likely cause is either UNDERFEEDING or TOO LITTLE LIGHT.

LEAVES DULL AND LIFELESS TOO MUCH LIGHT is the probable culprit; another possibility is RED SPIDER MITE. Even healthy green leaves can be rendered dull and lifeless by dust and grime.

BROWN TIPS OR EDGES ON LEAVES If edges remain green, the most likely cause is DRY AIR. Another possible reason is BRUISING — people or pets touching the tips can be the culprit, so can leaf tips pressing against a wall or window. If edges are yellow or brown, the possible causes are many and varied — OVERWATERING, UNDERWATERING, TOO LITTLE LIGHT, TOO MUCH SUN, TOO LITTLE HEAT, TOO MUCH HEAT, OVERFEEDING, DRY AIR or DRAUGHTS. To pinpoint the cause, look for other symptoms.

WILTING LEAVES The most usual cause is either SOIL DRYNESS (caused by underwatering) or WATERLOGGING (caused by impeded drainage or watering too frequently). Other possible causes are TOO MUCH LIGHT (especially if wilting takes place regularly at midday), DRY AIR, TOO MUCH HEAT, POT-BOUND ROOTS or PEST DAMAGE.

LEAF FALL ON NEW PLANTS It is quite normal for a newly repotted plant, a new purchase or a plant moved from one room to another, to lose one or two lower leaves. Keep MOVEMENT SHOCK to a minimum by repotting into a pot which is only slightly larger than the previous one, by protecting new plants on the way home from the shop and by never moving a plant from a shady spot to a very bright one without a few days in medium light.

NO FLOWERS If the plant has reached flowering size and blooms do not appear at the due time of year, several factors can be responsible. The most likely causes are lighting problems — TOO LITTLE LIGHT or WRONG DAYLENGTH. Other possibilities are OVERFEEDING, DRY AIR or REPOTTING (some flowering plants need to be pot-bound before they will flower).

FLOWERS QUICKLY FADE The commonest culprits are UNDERWATERING, DRY AIR, TOO LITTLE LIGHT and TOO MUCH HEAT.

HOLES AND TEARS IN LEAVES There are two basic causes — PHYSICAL DAMAGE by pets or people (merely brushing against an opening leaf bud can occasionally be responsible) or INSECT DAMAGE.

LOWER LEAVES DRY UP AND FALL There are three common causes — TOO LITTLE LIGHT, TOO MUCH HEAT or UNDERWATERING.

WHITE CRUST ON CLAY POT There are two possible causes — use of excessively HARD WATER or OVERFEEDING.

PESTS & DISEASES

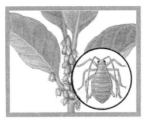

APHID (Greenfly)
Small, sap-sucking insects — green, black, grey or orange. All plants with soft tissues can be attacked. Flowering pot plants are especially susceptible. Spray with Flydown or Bio Sprayday — repeat as necessary

CATERPILLAR
A problem in the conservatory but rarely found on specimens in the living room. The tell-tale sign is the presence of holes in the leaves but some spin leaves together. Pick off and destroy individual caterpillars

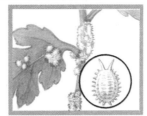

MEALY BUG
Small pests covered with white, cottony fluff. Large clusters can occur on the stems and under the leaves of a wide variety of plants. Wipe off with a damp cloth or spray with Flydown or a systemic insecticide

RED SPIDER MITE
Minute, sap-sucking pests which can infest the underside of leaves of nearly all house plants growing in hot and dry conditions. Leaves speckled on top, webbed below. Spray with Flydown or a systemic insecticide

SCALE
Small, brown discs attached to the underside of leaves, especially along the veins. Wipe off with a damp cloth and then spray the plant with Flydown or malathion. Severe infestations are difficult to eradicate

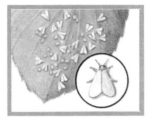

WHITEFLY
Tiny, moth-like insects which can be troublesome, especially to Begonia, Fuchsia, Impatiens and Pelargonium. The larvae suck sap and leaves may drop. Spray with Bio Sprayday at 3-day intervals

BOTRYTIS (Grey Mould)
Grey, fluffy mould which can cover all parts of the plant if the growing conditions are cool and humid. All soft-leaved plants can be affected. Cut away mouldy parts and spray with a systemic fungicide

CROWN & STEM ROT
Part of the stem or crown is soft and rotten — known as basal rot when the base of the plant is affected. Nearly always fatal — throw the plant away. In future avoid overwatering and keep the plant in a warmer place

POWDERY MILDEW
A white powdery deposit spotting or coating the surface of the leaves. Unlike Botrytis this disease is neither common nor fatal. Remove badly infected leaves — spray with a systemic fungicide

ROOT ROT (Tuber Rot)
A fatal disease to which Cacti, Succulents, Begonia, Palms and Saintpaulia are particularly prone. Yellowing and wilting of the leaves is followed by plant collapse. In future avoid over-watering

SOOTY MOULD
A black fungus which grows on the sticky honeydew which is deposited by aphid, scale, whitefly and mealy bug. Not particularly harmful — wipe off with a cloth and rinse with warm water

VIRUS
There is no single symptom of virus infection. The growth may be severely stunted and stems are often distorted. Yellow spots or blotches may appear on the leaves. There is no cure

SPRAYING

- **Use the right product** Make sure that it is recommended for the pest or disease to be controlled, and make sure that there is no warning against spraying the plant to be treated.
- **Buy a brand recommended for house plants** Where possible obtain a product which is specially recommended for use indoors — Bio Sprayday will not harm surrounding furnishings or fabrics.
- **Spray the right way** Before spraying read the instructions — avoid using too little or too much. Cover fish bowls and aquaria before you start. Spray thoroughly both above and below the leaves. Wash out the sprayer after use.
- **Spray the right plants** With the quick-moving invaders, such as aphid and whitefly, spray all the neighbouring plants. With slow-moving pests, such as scale and mealy bug, only plants which are infested need be sprayed.

Spraying Record

Date	Spray	Results

CHAPTER 4
DIARY

JANUARY

This is a resting period for most plants so water carefully — Cacti will not usually need any, Succulents just enough to prevent shrivelling. Several flowering plants should be in full bloom — Begonia, Primula, Poinsettia, Azalea, Cineraria, Christmas Cactus etc. When shoots have appeared bring the bowls of bulbs inside — place in a cool room.

FEBRUARY

Some plants are encouraged to start their growing cycle this month — Tuberous Begonias, Fuchsias etc. Others are now moving from their flowering to their resting period — Christmas Cactus, Indian Azalea etc. All the popular indoor bulbs are now in flower — Tulips, Hyacinths, Narcissi, Crocus and Lily of the Valley.

MARCH

March is the month for sowing many house plant seeds and for planting some tubers, e.g Gloxinia and Achimenes. Some pot plant bulbs such as Agapanthus are potted up now, but it is generally too early to take stem cuttings.

Look over your plants carefully as the growing season is about to begin. Remove dead or yellowing leaves and prick over the compost surface. Start to increase the frequency of watering if new growth is seen. Many bulbs will have come to the end of their active period — stop watering when leaves have withered. Remove bulbs, allow to dry and store.

APRIL

The resting period is now over and so feeding and more frequent watering are required. Some plants will require repotting — consult The House Plant Expert to see whether it is advisable for the plants you grow. Pot-bound plants have to be repotted — check by carefully removing the soil ball from the pot and looking for a mass of matted roots on the outside. This is the symptom of a pot-bound plant.

Cuttings of varieties which root readily can be taken this month — examples include Impatiens, Hedera and Hydrangea. For most varieties, however, it is better to wait until June or July.

MAY

The sunlight is now stronger and so it will be necessary to shade windowsill plants from the midday sun. Most plants will be growing rapidly — nip out the growing points of straggly shoots to keep plants bushy and tie climbers to supports.

The summer show of flowering plants begins this month — look for the Hoyas, Spathiphyllum, Begonia semperflorens, Regal Pelargonium, Streptocarpus and many others. Watering and feeding should now be at the summer rate — fresh air is needed by many plants but watch out for draughts.

JUNE

Continue watering and feeding at the summer rate. On hot and dry days mist the leaves to increase the humidity. On showery days many plants benefit from a short spell outdoors. Pests often make their appearance in June — keep watch for aphids and whitefly. Tackle outbreaks promptly.

This is the peak season for taking cuttings — see page 56. June is also the time for sowing seeds of spring-flowering plants such as Calceolaria and Cineraria. The summer flower show is enriched by Tuberous Begonias and Bougainvillea.

JULY

All the summer jobs described for June will be necessary this month. You may have to water even more frequently. Increase humidity by misting — an alternative technique (see page 54) may have to be used.

This month marks the start of the holiday season and this is a period of strain for your plants. Move the plants out of the sun and water them thoroughly. If you can, surround the pots with moist peat. Ask a friend to call in occasionally to water the plants if your holiday is due to last more than 10 days.

AUGUST

Continue watering and feeding at the summer rate. If your holidays are planned for this month, take the precautions described for July. This is the last of the peak months for striking cuttings, although you can wait until September for Fuchsias, Pelargonium and the Ivies.

August marks the start of the bulb-planting season. There are Zantedeschia and some other exotics, but by far the most popular ones are the Narcissi. Follow the rules to avoid disappointment — see The House Plant Expert.

SEPTEMBER

It is now time to look ahead to winter. You can buy Cyclamen for late autumn display and there are all the bulbs to plant (Tulips, Hyacinths, Narcissi etc) for winter and early spring display.

Both watering and feeding will need to be slightly reduced. Sun-loving plants should be moved to a brighter spot and cold-sensitive plants should be moved away from cold windows. Continue to watch for pests — red spider mite can be a problem at this time of year. Finish plant-disturbing jobs such as pruning and repotting.

OCTOBER

Watering must be reduced for plants which rest during the winter — look up the plant in the Varieties section to see the water requirement during the October to March period. Complete planting bowls of bulbs.

The summer display of flowers is now over but these days there is no shortage of blooms at any time of the year — Pot Chrysanthemums, Begonias, African Violets etc. Wash the leaves of foliage plants if dust has collected on them during the summer months.

NOVEMBER

Winter generally arrives this month and it is a trying time for many plants. Watering should now be at the winter level and where possible the pots should be moved to the recommended winter quarters. Many plants need cool but bright conditions in winter.

The cycle of warm days and cold nights is intolerable for many plants — central heating helps to overcome this problem. Unfortunately central heating dries out the air — so remember to mist the plants as recommended. Buying plants at this time of the year can pose a risk — see page 50.

DECEMBER

A peak month for buying house plants for Christmas decoration and as gifts. Vast numbers of Poinsettia, Solanum, Azalea, Cyclamen and African Violet are purchased. Follow the cultural recommendations carefully — they have widely differing needs.

Continue to water carefully, provide extra light if possible and satisfy the minimum temperature requirement. Review the notes you have made in the Varieties section, and make a list of the plants you want to try next year.

DIARY

CHAPTER 5
INDEX

INDEX

Acknowledgements
The author wishes to acknowledge the painstaking work of Gill Jackson, Jane Llewelyn and John Woodbridge. Grateful acknowledgement is also made to Constance Barry, Joan Hessayon, Linda Fensom and Angelina Gibbs. Henry Barnett prepared the paintings for this book. Other artists who contributed were June Baker, Norman Barber, Mike Standage and Yvon Still.